# MANAGING NEW MUSEUMS

## A GUIDE TO GOOD PRACTICE

TIMOTHY AMBROSE

SCOTTISH
MUSEUMS
COUNCIL

EDINBURGH : HMSO

© Crown Copyright 1993

First Published as *New Museums - A Start-up Guide,* 1987

This edition, first published 1993

British Library Cataloguing in Publication Data

A catalogue record for this book is available from the British Library


The Scottish Museums Council is an independent company,
principally funded by the Secretary of State for Scotland. The
Council's mission is to improve the quality of museum and gallery
provision in Scotland. This it seeks to do by providing a wide range
of advice, services and financial assistance to its membership, and
representing the interests of museums in Scotland.


Scottish Museums Council

County House

20-22 Torphichen Street

Edinburgh

EH3 8JB


tel. 031-229 7465    fax. 031–229 2728

ISBN 0 11 495157 8

# PREFACE

The first edition of this book was published in 1987 under the title *New Museums - A Start-up Guide*. The publishers invited me to produce a revised edition in 1992. I was pleased to accept the invitation for three reasons. Firstly, it has allowed me to correct some small errors in the first edition; secondly, it has given me the opportunity to include references to new developments and publications which have appeared in the past five years in the museums world; and thirdly, it has provided me with a chance to re-order the emphasis of the book on managing new museums, rather than setting them up. At the same time I hope that the book will nonetheless continue to be of benefit to those who are thinking seriously of establishing a new museum.

The structure of the book has thus been revised to allow for this new emphasis to be made and to address a UK market rather than a predominantly Scottish one. All of the sections have been revised and brought up-to-date where changes have occurred, and a number of new sections have been added.

The book was revised during the winter of 1992 and I would like to thank the publishers, in particular Dr Susan Hemmings, for their help and encouragement throughout the process. I am also indebted to my colleagues in the Scottish Museums Council and its sister Area Museum Councils in England, Wales and Northern Ireland for their help through discussion and critical comment. My thanks are also due to the many people working in museums and other organisations throughout the UK who have answered questions on developments in their area and made comments on the draft text. For what you are about to read however, I must take ultimate responsibility.

Timothy Ambrose

# CONTENTS

# INTRODUCTION
## ABOUT THIS BOOK

In the past twenty years or so there has been a remarkable growth of interest in developing new museums throughout the UK. *Managing New Museums* has been written for those managing new museums or considering setting up a new museum. It is not a blue-print for a new museum, nor is it a do-it-yourself guide to managing museums. Instead, it examines the many different responsibilities which go with managing new and successful museums, and seeks to answer some of the common questions raised by those involved in museum developments particularly in the independent sector. *Managing New Museums* has been designed to be read straight through to give an overview of setting up and managing a new museum. It can also be used as a basic guide and checklist when the reader is confronted with particular problems. It should not be seen however as a substitute for direct and specific professional advice.

*Managing New Museums* is arranged in four main sections. The opening section - *First Steps* - poses some general questions for the would-be or new museum manager, and describes some of the help available in answering those questions. The second section - *Managing the Collections* - details the ways in which museums form and care for their collections. *The Museum and its Users*, the third section, examines the range of services provided for the museum's users and their effective marketing. The final section - *Managing the Museum* - describes the various management responsibilities for staff and governing bodies which go with new museum ventures.

No book of this type can pretend to be comprehensive. In some cases it touches on areas of work, in others it goes into greater detail. Follow-up reading is given in *Further Reading,* and *Other Sources of Information* provides guidance on additional assistance. If you wish to follow up in more detail any of the matters raised in the book you should contact your Area Museum Council in the first instance. Their staff will be pleased to help you.

# FIRST STEPS

*'We had no idea of the amount of work needed to set up and run a new museum when we started. If we'd known then what we know now, I doubt very much whether we would have been so ambitious!'*

## 1.1 WHAT IS A MUSEUM? - SOME DEFINITIONS

There is perhaps surprisingly no universally agreed definition of a museum. Given the very wide range of sizes and types of institutions which are called museums, this is perhaps not too surprising. Here are three definitions currently in use:

### (a) The International Council of Museums (ICOM)

The International Council of Museums defines a museum as a 'non-profit making, permanent institution, in the service of society and of its development, and open to the public, which acquires, conserves, researches and communicates, and exhibits, for the purpose of study, education and enjoyment, material evidence of people and their environment.'

The Council also recognises that the following may fall under this definition:

Conservation institutes and exhibition galleries permanently maintained by libraries and archive centres;

Natural, archaeological and ethnographic monuments and sites and historical monuments and sites of a museum nature, for their acquisition, conservation and communication activities;

Institutions displaying live specimens, such as botanic and zoological gardens, aquaria, vivaria, etc;

Nature reserves;

Science centres and planetaria.

This is a fairly wide-ranging definition. It encompasses institutions which in the public mind might not normally be viewed as museums.

### (b) The Museums Association (MA)

The Museums Association defines a museum in much simpler terms as 'an institution which collects, documents, preserves, exhibits and interprets material evidence and associated information for the public benefit'. This definition has been used by the Museums and Galleries Commission in its national Museum Registration scheme (see section 4.5).

The Museums Association explains its definition as follows:

**Institution** implies a formalised establishment which has a long-term purpose;

**Collects** embraces all means of acquisition;

**Documents** emphasises the need to maintain records;

**Preserves** includes all aspects of conservation and security;

**Exhibits** confirms the expectation of visitors that they will be able to see at least a representative selection of objects in the collection;

**Interprets** covers such diverse fields as display, education, research and publication;

**Material** indicates something that is tangible;

**Evidence** guarantees its authenticity as the real thing;

**Associated information** represents the knowledge which prevents a museum object merely being a curio, and also includes all records relating to its past history, acquisition and subsequent usage;

**For the public benefit** is deliberately open-ended and is intended to reflect current thinking that museums are servants of society.

### (c) The Museum Training Institute (MTI)

The Museum Training Institute's definition of the key purpose of a museum is:

> 'to acquire, preserve, research, exhibit and communicate material evidence and associated information of people and the environment for learning and enjoyment'.

In all of these definitions you will note that there is an emphasis on collections and their management. Collections and the responsibilities which go with them are what differentiate museums fundamentally from other interpretive facilities such as heritage centres, visitor centres or exhibition centres which are not collections-based. In a number of cases the term *heritage centre* has been used for marketing reasons to describe a facility which is functionally a museum. Some 50% of all heritage centres in the UK are in fact museums! The remainder present their stories or messages using a variety of media, but do not seek to manage and interpret collections. The term has

Collections and the responsibilities which go with them are what differentiates museums fundamentally from other interpretive facilities such as heritage centres, visitor centres or exhibition centres which are not collections-based.

gained currency in recent years with the growth of public interest in the cultural and natural heritage and its interpretation. It is important at an early stage in new museum developments to be clear about the core functions and responsibilities of museums, and the differences between collections-based institutions and non-collections-based institutions (see section 1.3).

Whatever name a museum is described by in the market-place - and there is no reason not to use the term 'museum' in describing your facility if it is carrying out the functions of a museum and has been established to do so - staff, management, users and supporters should all be clear about its functions and responsibilities.

## 1.2 MUSEUMS IN THE UNITED KINGDOM

Within the last two decades museums have turned into a major growth area within the leisure and tourism industry and are playing an increasingly important part in this sector of the economy.

Museums of all type - national, local authority, independent, university, regimental - in the different parts of the United Kingdom now attract some 100 million visits each year. In Scotland alone for example, almost 10 million visits to museums are made annually. Within the last two decades museums have turned into a major growth area within the leisure and tourism industry and are playing an increasingly important part in this sector of the economy.

The root causes of this groundswell of interest in museums are not difficult to understand. First, the pace of change in society has quickened since the Second World War and the rapid growth of new technologies has affected many traditional patterns of economic and social life. It is not surprising that there has been corresponding reaction against such change. For many particularly older visitors, museums can seem to provide a sense of permanence and stability. They can help to demonstrate continuity in the face of change and reaffirm traditional values. In a very real sense the past is enlisted to combat the present. Many new museums particularly in the independent sector are established not by the young but by older members of the community who wish to record and preserve something of their past in the face of change.

Secondly, the scale and rate of destruction of the environment since the War has given rise to a powerful conservation movement. The realisation of the loss to the nation's cultural and natural heritage has encouraged a greater and more informed interest in the environment, both natural and man-made. This has in turn led to a greater interest in participation and involvement in the conservation movement at national, regional and local level. A wide range of media has been brought into play to present both the heritage itself and the case for its care and conservation to an ever-growing and ever-more knowledgeable audience. Museums can be viewed as one of these media.

Thirdly, in recent years the United Kingdom has moved away from its traditional manufacturing economy towards a service economy. Leisure and tourism services and facilities have developed in response to increased leisure time, improved standards of living for many, and more disposable income. The establishment of new museums, and redevelopment and renewal programmes in existing museums as they have responded to an increasingly competitive market, have reflected these changes.

The number of museums catering for the new leisure markets has consequently grown. Building on an already rich and diverse pattern of provision, new museums, in parallel with other heritage facilities, have sprung up throughout the UK to cater for this upsurge in interest and demand. Many of our new museums have been developed within the independent sector, usually with local and/or central government support. Many, although not all, have set new standards in the quality of their presentation and the range of services on offer to their public, which has become increasingly sophisticated in its level of expectation. This has also had a knock-on effect in existing public sector museums, many of long standing, which have had to take these new standards into account in their own renewal and development programmes.

Altogether there are some 2500 museums in the UK, 1300 of which are in the independent sector. The pattern of development has varied from area to area depending on the nature and extent of existing provision. In Scotland for example, some 200 new museums out of a total of 400 have been set up in the last 15-20 years both by local authorities and independent organisations. New museums in the last two to three decades have generally, although not exclusively, concentrated on nineteenth- and twentieth-century history. Particularly noticeable growth has been in museums presenting aspects of Britain's industrial history, and in small community-based museums in rural and urban areas.

Such development has been largely unplanned and motivated in the main by local considerations. In a number of cases, despite the caveats raised in section 1.4, some museums have been set up without due regard to their relationship with existing museums, or sufficient clarity of thought about their long-term management or funding. The average number of visitors to each museum has also been dropping over the past ten to fifteen years as more museums enter what some would consider to be an increasingly over-crowded marketplace. Later sections of this book look at the range of a museum's responsibilities and demonstrate how important effective pre-planning and feasibility assessment is to a museum's future success.

Some museums have been set up without due regard to their relationship with existing museums, or sufficient clarity of thought about their long-term management or funding.

## 1.3 WHAT DO MUSEUMS DO?

It would be easy to answer this question simply by reference to section 1.1 (b) above, where the key functions of a museum are defined. Museums are however, more complex organisations than this common definition would seem to imply. In the first instance while all museums will be able to recognise themselves in this basic definition, the range of museums is extremely wide. At one end of the spectrum are the great national museums with substantial numbers of professional staff like the British Museum, the National Museum of Wales, the Royal Museum of Scotland or the Ulster Museum; at the other end, lie tiny, community museums run by community groups in rural and remote areas of the UK. While this functional definition may be shared, in the same way as a London department store and a corner-shop in Belfast are both shops, the scale and complexity of their operation is dramatically different. Because of these differences in scale - whether with reference to budgets, buildings, staffing, collections or user numbers - it follows that a simple answer to the question - what do museums do? - is not possible.

Despite these differences however there are some general points about museums which do hold good across the spectrum. First, all museums, whatever their size, are collections-based. Their collections, both three-dimensional and two-dimensional, including audio and visual material, provide the public with opportunities to confront original material related to the cultural and natural heritage. Those collections span all human endeavour and the natural world. They are not confined to the UK, and many museums hold collections from different parts of the world. They can be more or less specialised depending on the nature and type of museum holding them. Museums of all type therefore have a primary responsibility to care for and manage those collections. Collecting, documenting, preserving and conserving collections take up a large part of a museum's work.

Collecting may range from full-scale archaeological research excavations or plant-collecting expeditions abroad, to one-off donations of items which have been 'in the family' for years. Documenting may be a relatively straightforward task of entering information about an object acquired by the museum into the museum's computerised documentation system, or a complex task requiring a significant amount of specialised research and scientific investigation. Preserving similarly may be a question of keeping an object in a secure, controlled environment in an existing storage area, or managing the development of large-scale industrial-type warehousing for a collection of steam trains. Conserving can cover specialist remedial conservation work on any type of object in a museum collection, of whatever scale from steamships through to Roman coins, elephants through to beetles. Much will depend on the scale and type of museum and the nature of the collections it holds; but all have to meet the same functional responsibilities associated with managing collections.

In a very real sense, museums are not buildings - they are collections. Without a collection, you do not have a museum.

The second point in answer to the question - what do museums do? - is their relationship with the public. Museums do not manage their collections for themselves but for the public. Again, the scale and type of museum will determine the range of public services which a museum can provide, and we explore some of these in the various sections of this book. They include education services, leisure learning programmes, oral history recording, reminiscence work with the elderly, displays and exhibitions, publications, and lectures carried out within the museum and outside it, often in partnership with other organisations. To be successful, museums have to be active organisations, and should not be confused with static exhibitions.

In a very real sense, museums are not buildings - they are collections. Without a collection, you do not have a museum.

Exhibitions and displays form but one part of museums' work, and it is the full range of their relationship with the public which has to be considered in examining what they do. They exist for the public benefit, not commercial gain. Their collections are held in trust for the public, not as commercial assets. The profit motive exists only so far as earned income can support the museum's responsibilities to its collections and to its public.

The third point is that museums provide cultural and social, economic and political benefits to the communities which support them. They help to enhance the quality of people's lives and provide a sense of identity for their area; the act as a cultural focus contributing to the cultural infrastructure and providing a wide range of cultural activities of value to their users; they support economic development programmes providing a focus with other facilities and services for inward investment and employment; and they foster a sense of local pride and belonging, of particular importance in multi-ethnic communities. Benefits such as these can be thought of in quantitative or qualitative terms, but together they demonstrate that what museums do goes a long way beyond a simple functional description. In managing your new museum, it is worthwhile ensuring that the benefits which your museum does provide are identified within any case for support which you are making to external organisations.

## 1.4 ALTERNATIVE APPROACHES

If you are interested in interpreting the cultural or natural history of a place or area, it is easy to jump to the conclusion that the development of a museum is the only way to meet your aims. It may be, but it may also *not* be. Quite often an alternative approach can be more appropriate and more cost-effective.

For example, the story of a local town or village or area can be explored in a wide variety of different ways using many different media:

>    a series of leaflets

>    a pictorial history book

>    an illustrated map

>    a series of postcards

sets of slide-packs with notes

a tape-slide programme

a video

an educational resource pack

a series of audio-cassettes

an historical novel

display boards

a self-guided trail

dramatic reconstructions of past events

a son-et-lumière presentation

a festival

guided walks or bus tours

a temporary exhibition

a network of site interpretation points

*etc.*

A combination of such approaches might be equally appropriate. A museum may not be the relevant medium for your purposes at all!

Many proposals for new museums do not stem from the existence of an important collection, or the feeling that some vital element of local history has been overlooked or is endangered, but rather from the fact that an interesting historic building has become available or is threatened with destruction. As we will see, the establishment of a museum whatever the size, has to be carefully and critically assessed in terms of the long-term responsibilities it must shoulder.

The establishment of a museum whatever the size, has to be carefully and critically assessed in terms of the long-term responsibilities it must shoulder.

It is all too often the case that a wave of infectious enthusiasm enables a new museum to be set up and to be run perhaps successfully for a few years until a clearer understanding of the basic, on-going responsibilities begins to dawn. Everyone loves to collect objects and make displays - in far fewer cases is there an interest in carefully documenting those objects, cleaning and storing them in appropriate conditions, acting as voluntary guides, dealing with correspondence and financial accounts and maintaining a possibly old and adapted building year after year. The enthusiastic band of people who set up the museum are not always the best people to manage a museum for the long-term - different skills are usually needed.

## 1.5 SETTING UP A NEW MUSEUM

Feasibility assessment is a vital step to ensuring long-term viability and success. It is best carried out not by the person(s) wishing to establish a museum or museum service, but by specialist consultants with a wide range of experience in this field working in close conjunction with their clients.

The advantages of this approach are two-fold. First, professional consultants have a wide range of experience and expertise and can draw on relevant examples of good practice to support their recommendations. They can thus provide an independent and objective assessment of the project. Secondly, a detailed feasibility study provides a sound basis on which to approach funding and other support agencies to seek their help. A feasibility assessment essentially secures the project credibility, and also has the benefit of alerting the promoters to the range of responsibilities which they will need to shoulder and the short-, medium-, and long-term commitments to be undertaken.

### Questions to be asked

A feasibility study will ask the following questions:

What market exists for your proposed museum and its services? Who are your potential visitors? When will they visit the museum? How many will come in any one year, month, week, day? What will they want from the museum? How will you attract them back again? What museums and other facilities will you be in competition with?

What themes are to be explored by the museum?

How are they to be researched? Who will carry out and coordinate the background research? Is he/she appropriately qualified and experienced? Is the information readily available

*Feasibility assessment is a vital step to ensuring long-term viability and success.*

or dispersed in libraries, record offices, museums etc? Is the information to be gathered reliable and accurate? Is it up-to-date? How long will a research programme take to complete? How much will it cost?

What collections are available to illustrate these themes? Who owns them? Has a preliminary audit been carried out of the potential collections and their historical value? How will they be acquired/developed? What skills do you have in terms of their effective care and interpretation?

How are these themes best presented - through displays, exhibitions, tableaux, publications, audio-visual presentations, information technology, guided tours, or activity centres?

What range of activities will be carried out in the museum e.g. individual and group visits, exhibitions, displays, educational activities, storage of reserve collections, documentation of collections, office work, staff rest-breaks, meetings, eating and drinking, etc?

What size and quality of space is required within the museum to accommodate all of these activities e.g. environmentally stable storage, display and exhibition space, office space, meetings room(s), rest rooms, toilets, sales and information points?

What spaces are required outside the museum e.g. car-parking space, entrance ramps, picnic areas, loading bays etc?

What buildings are required to house the chosen functions? What standard of buildings are required? Should the museum be housed in new or old building(s)?

Are buildings originally earmarked for museum use really suitable for the task in hand?

What is the nature of the organisation best suited to manage the museum e.g. an incorporated or unincorporated body, a local authority, a joint board, professional or volunteer staff?

What skills are required to manage the museum and its operations? Are appropriate individuals available within the local community to carry out the necessary work? What training will they need? How will they familiarise themselves with appropriate standards of museum practice?

What are the costs involved in capital and revenue terms? What are the setting up costs? How much will the museum cost to run each year? How will it be heated? How will the environment for collections on display or in storage be controlled? How much money will be needed to change displays/exhibitions, document and store the collections, pay staff and volunteers, maintain the fabric of the building(s)?

What are the economic benefits to be gained from the establishment of the new museum? What other organisations will benefit from your presence and activities - hotels, garages, restaurants, coach and bus firms? How many new jobs will be created in the museum and in the vicinity? What scale of visitor spend is anticipated at other facilities?

What will be the relationship to museums and other facilities which already exist in the area or elsewhere? Which professional bodies will the museum be expected to work with?

What is the nature of the development programme needed to meet the museum's aims? Over what length of time and at what pace does the museum need to programme its development? How will it meet Museum Registration standards and thus be eligible for public funding support?

What sources of funding would be available to the museum, for example tourist organisations, Area Museum Councils, Museums and Galleries Commission, enterprise councils or agencies, private sector/charitable organisations, local authorities?

What action would be required to secure funding for the development programme for example drawing up a fund-raising programme and producing promotional materials; appointing fund-raising consultants or forming a committee; or launching an appeal?

Last, but not least - is the venture feasible and will it be viable for the long-term? Is it really necessary?

## Defining purpose

Having determined that the establishment of a museum is feasible and the necessary and appropriate course of action, the next step is to analyse its fundamental purpose. The aims and values of the new institution need to be considered in depth at the very outset of thinking and planning. They will not only determine the nature of the museum itself, but influence all aspects of the museum's subsequent development. It is necessary for the museum's management, staff, volunteers, funding agencies, and the museum's users to all know what the museum's purpose is - after all, they will all be contributing in different ways to help the museum realise its objectives.

A definition of purpose or mission statement will differ from institution to institution. Some examples might be - to preserve and interpret the history of a local community; to increase and deepen public understanding of the historical development of a town or a district; to interpret the historical and natural environment of a particular area; to promote and realise the educational potential of a particular collection; to provide an educational resource for the local community, etc. All of these essentially represent statements of intent. Once the museum's purpose or mission has been agreed, the way is then open to analyse what its functional objectives should be, to establish policies for the museum's work in the light of these objectives (see section 1.11), and then to draw up a programme of action in the shape of a forward plan. The museum's functional objectives will subsume the functions of a museum given in section 1.1.

## Specialist consultants

Many of the questions about feasibility above require detailed research and familiarity with existing museum provision in the UK. There are considerable benefits to be gained in employing specialists in this kind of appraisal work. On the one hand it makes the organisation promoting a new museum face up to the realities of museum work and understand the context within which the museum will be operating. On the other hand, it helps to provide a coherent and fully argued case-for-support to potential supporters. Area Museum Councils are well placed to provide details of suitable consultants for your project, and to assist in their recruitment and selection.

The aims and values of the new institution need to be considered in depth at the very outset of thinking and planning.

Many of the questions about feasibility require detailed research and familiarity with existing museum provision in the UK.

13

## 1.6 TESTING THE WATER

One practical method of helping to assess feasibility which a local group promoting the idea of a new museum might use is to set up a 'temporary museum' programme. This can be used to gauge the level of local visitor and tourist visitor interest. Your 'museum' might consist of a number of short-term elements and activities designed to 'test the water'. This is known as formative evaluation and assists in identifying successful practice. Here is a sample approach and programme:

A local group decided to discover what sort of interest in community history could be developed by setting up what they called a 'history shop'. The aim of the shop was to encourage people to drop in to discuss a specific theme with volunteer staff and to make a record of their experience. The theme chosen was appropriately enough 'shopping' and the location of the history shop was on the High Street of the local town in premises specially rented from the local authority for the purpose. Rent and rates were paid for through joint sponsorship by the local business community and a fund-raising exercise.

The volunteers who staffed the history shop all worked to the same brief and had a short, but intensive, training programme before they began work. They recorded individuals' experiences of changes in local shops and shopping , goods and services, weights and measures, and currency on audiotape, questionnaires and videofilm. At the same time they investigated what original 2-dimensional and 3-dimensional material relating to the theme was available in private ownership. They planned to draw on this database for later exhibition purposes. Much of this material was documented in detail on computer and photographed and then returned to its owners. The group carried out a research programme on the architecture of local shops and arranged a series of interviews with shopkeepers to obtain their views from the other side of the counter.

The archive of information was then used as a basis for developing an exhibition on the theme of shops and shopping. The exhibition was designed to tour to a number of local venues, including schools, community halls and local libraries in the area. Discussion groups and workshops were held at several of these and more information was fed back into the database. Of particular interest were the different attitudes to shopping shown by people living in the town compared with those living in the surrounding countryside.

In parallel with this project, a booklet was prepared and later published on the history of shops and shopping in the town. The sales of the booklet provided additional revenue income for the group. The overall exercise was repeated for three years with different themes until it was clear that there existed sufficient public interest in the project and sufficient local collections to warrant considering a more permanent facility.

Some of the fundamental lessons learnt from this exercise were that to maintain public interest in the venture the group needed to:

> encourage and seek active participation in the fact-finding process from local people;
>
> provide an easily accessible point for people to drop into to discuss past and present experiences of shopping;
>
> develop a range of events and activities in association with the central project to extend interest;
>
> produce an end-product - in this case an exhibition and publication - to demonstrate in tangible terms the value of individual contributions;
>
> be prepared to give much time and energy to ensure the success of the project.

In the case study above, the group developed a range of experience and skills which gave them an insight into what managing a permanent museum might require. The group covered such tasks as project planning and development, fund-raising, publicity and promotion, fieldwork and research, computerised information recording, photographic recording, collections documentation, community involvement, managing premises, exhibition planning, design and production, organisation of associated events and activities, and evaluation and assessment. They were able to measure their achievements and competence against the standards developed for museums by the Museum Training Institute.

A great deal was therefore learnt by the group about its capabilities and also about the nature of some of the tasks for the future. Of equal importance was the fact that no long-term investment had been made in a new museum before a clearer understanding of its management had been gained. Experience of this type can be used to enhance a later feasibility assessment for a permanent facility.

This is but one demonstration of how the water might be tested before taking the plunge to establish a new museum. It goes some way towards demonstrating the type of commitment required in managing a museum if it is to be a success. There are many other ways, some more, some less ambitious. Testing the water should provide experience of as many different facets of setting up and managing a museum as possible.

*Testing the water should provide experience of as many different facets of setting up and managing a museum as possible.*

## 1.7 RESOURCES

What are the key resources needed in setting up and managing a new museum? In broad terms there are six - collections, premises, people, money, time, and equipment. All of these are interdependent.

### Collections

A museum without collections is no museum at all. Collections after all are the main reason for a museum being in existence (see section 1.1). It is surprisingly common to find that an appraisal of what can be collected within the theme(s) of the museum has not been carried out as an integral part of planning a new museum, but almost as an afterthought. The interest of a museum lies essentially in the collections it cares for and makes available to users, and their significance.

*It is surprisingly common to find that an appraisal of what can be collected within the theme(s) of the museum has not been carried out as an integral part of planning a new museum, but almost as an afterthought.*

If the collections are inadequate or of little consequence or significance, then it can be strongly argued that the capital and revenue investment in a museum to house and display them is really not worthwhile. Considerable attention needs to be applied to the formation of collections at an early stage of feasibility assessment for a new museum.

It should always be remembered that every item acquired for the collections carries a cost implication in terms of its documentation, storage, display, management and security. A museum therefore has to justify acquiring and managing items for its collections in both financial as well as academic terms.

## Premises

Premises are another key resource. Adequate housing for the collections and the activities to be undertaken by the museum is vital. Much attention has to be given to the suitability of existing buildings for the whole range of functions which are to be carried out (see section 1.5). Premises being viewed from the point of view of museum use should be assessed not simply in terms of display and exhibition use.

To take one example, storage - it is quite common in new museum developments to find that no space, or insufficient space, has been allocated in initial plans for reserve collections. These are collections held by the museum which are not on display or in use. As much care and attention needs to be devoted to the storage of collections as their display. If collections are housed in inadequate storage, they are at risk and the museum is not meeting its responsibilities to the collections or to the people who donated them to the museum. A high standard of preventive conservation for collections in storage, or on display, means that the museum will not incur the often sizeable costs of remedial conservation at a later date (see section 2.4).

Where new museum buildings are being planned, the key to success lies in briefing architects effectively so that the needs of the museum can be appropriately met (see section 4.2). Good quality new buildings cannot guarantee good quality museums, but they should provide considerable savings in time and expense in the long term if they have been designed to carry out the museum functions from the start.

## People

People represent another important resource - for management, for staffing, for fund-raising and for support. The range of experience of those setting up and managing a new museum is a vital consideration in management planning. The composition of a Board of Trustees or management committee, for example, will play an important role in ensuring that the necessary expertise and skills are brought to bear at the right time and in the right place. The capabilities of the individuals on a museum's governing body can be an extremely valuable resource, which, if 'bought in', could be prohibitively expensive e.g. financial advice, management advice, marketing advice, professional curatorial support (see section 4.1).

It will almost certainly be important to develop the individuals involved in the museum through appropriate training programmes to ensure that they can make a useful as well as an enthusiastic contribution to the museum (see section 4.8). The new occupational standards for the museums, galleries and heritage sector developed by the Museum Training Institute are an important benchmark for training programmes in new museums.

Active volunteers may well need to be trained in the tasks which they are being asked to carry out, building on the skills which they already possess.

Other support groups, such as Friends' organisations, will need to be kept informed of progress. If they are involved in activities like fund-raising or events programmes, members will require a close understanding of the museum's aims, policies and objectives in the particular areas in which they are involved.

In these and other ways it is possible to help and encourage people to contribute to the museum in practical and useful ways. Maintaining and managing an effective group of volunteers or supporters is both a necessary and time-consuming task. The management and organisational skills needed should not be underestimated.

## Money

In general terms a museum is going to require financial support in two main areas - *capital* and *revenue*

Money is of course one of the first resources to spring to mind. The different approaches to raising funds for the establishment and management of a new museum are outlined at section 4.4. In general terms a museum is going to require financial support in two main areas - *capital* and *revenue*. Money for capital expenditure i.e. one-off costs such as building work, displays, or equipment can be comparatively easy to obtain. Giving funds for something tangible is more appealing to supporters than providing funds towards the running or operating costs (revenue expenditure) of a museum. Continuous commitment of this sort is more difficult to obtain. This is an essential fact to bear in mind in developing and managing new museums. The running costs of a new museum are often underestimated, and areas of responsibility such as collections management suffer in consequence.

*Revenue income* will be needed not simply to cope with the running costs and staffing of a museum, but also to carry out such essential tasks as conservation, documentation, storage, exhibition work and marketing. In setting up and managing new museums, it is of critical importance to draw up realistic revenue budget estimates and cash-flow forecasts as part of any feasibility assessment (see section 4.3).

## Time

The use and availability of people's time is a resource which should be considered from the outset of new museum development. It is again surprising how often organisations and individuals setting up and managing new museums greatly underestimate the amount of time needed to carry out their development programme. It is not uncommon to talk to people who imagine that a museum can be 'put together' satisfactorily in a matter of weeks. An instant museum is rarely, if ever, an instant success!

A carefully thought through and structured forward plan with adequate and realistic time assigned for the tasks ahead and sufficient inbuilt flexibility to allow for the unforeseen is an essential management tool. Effective time management plays a key part in ensuring that a museum meets its objectives.

> A carefully thought through and structured forward plan with adequate and realistic time assigned for the tasks ahead and sufficient inbuilt flexibility to allow for the unforeseen is an essential management tool.

## Equipment

Lastly, the range of equipment a museum holds will usually be built up over a period of years. There are no hard and fast rules, and some items of equipment will be regarded as essential by some but not by others. Equipment designed to monitor and control environmental conditions where original material is being displayed or stored is an important resource to invest in; this will enable staff to ensure the safekeeping of collections.

> Equipment designed to monitor and control environmental conditions where original material is being displayed or stored is an important resource to invest in.

Other equipment may include computers, office equipment and furniture, storage materials and lifting equipment, workshop tools, cleaning materials, disaster kits, first-aid equipment, display/exhibition systems, etc. Much depends on the scale and nature of your museum. In drawing up detailed budgets, it will be necessary to decide what will have to be acquired and when within the museum's development programme.

As with all museum work, a useful step to take is to talk with people working in other similar museums and discuss what they have found essential or useful in their work.

## 1.8 AREA MUSEUM COUNCILS (AMCs)

The ten Area Museum Councils in the UK are museum partnerships. Their members include almost all of the 2500 museums in the UK. The Councils promote excellence by fostering self-help and cooperation, by providing services to their members and by offering grant-aid for improvement projects and programmes. They are all independent companies with charitable status, answerable to their membership. They are principally funded by central government, but increasingly supplement their grant-in-aid with fees from services and funding from external sources in the private and public sector. The seven regional Area Museum Councils in England receive their grant-in-aid through the Museums and Galleries Commission (MGC) from the Department of National Heritage, while those in Scotland, Wales and Northern Ireland receive their funding direct through the Scottish, Welsh and Northern Ireland Offices.

Area Museum Councils have an overview of the museums within their areas from the largest local authority museum service to the smallest independent volunteer-run museum. They offer advisory services for organisations seeking to establish new museums, and for museums developing existing services. They provide financial support through targeted grants, usually on a matching basis, in support of projects which are designed to improve standards of care for their collections and standards of care for their users. Help with operational costs is not provided, although pump-priming grants for professional posts may be provided.

An important part of the Area Museum Councils' work is helping museums look after their collections. They help with advice on preventive conservation and provide access to remedial conservation services either through their own conservators or by arrangement with other conservators in the private or public sector. Conservation work is highly specialised and the Councils enable smaller museum which do not have their own laboratories to gain access to high quality conservation services.

All of the Area Museum Councils place a high priority on training across the whole range of museum activities from volunteer to senior manager. Most provide their own training programmes, as well as financial support for people working in museums to take up training opportunities. They work closely with other training providers and the Museum Training Institute to ensure training programmes are standards-based and help individuals improve their skills and competence in the work-place.

Their staff provide day-to-day advice on professional matters to their members and other organisations. Many have information services and libraries making available published material on museum work to their members, and circulating information on museum matters to their members through newsletters and mailings.

Area Museum Councils also provide marketing services to help museums increase their existing audiences and to develop new ones. Other services include helping museums develop or extend their public services. Some provide design and display services, others hire out touring exhibitions with the aims of getting new collections on show and encouraging repeat visits to museums. All Area Museum Councils are involved with museum education, actively helping museums meet the demands of the new schools' curricula and developing informal education programmes within museums.

Another important part of the Councils' work is advocacy. Representing the interests and needs of their members is an important role. They play an important part in promoting coherent and cost-effective museum services. They work in partnership with the Museums and Galleries Commission in administering the national Museum Registration scheme (see section 4.5). They are actively involved with museum planning and hold regular discussions with local authorities, regional and national agencies and other organisations with interests in museum developments. They are increasingly becoming involved in European museum networks and working in partnership with other European museum advisory services.

For all those managing or setting up new museums, Area Museum Councils represent an important source of practical help and advice. Early and continuing contact with your Area Museum Council is strongly advised and highly recommended (see section 6.0 for a list of Area Museum Councils and contact information).

For all those managing or setting up new museums, Area Museum Councils represent an important source of practical help and advice.

## 1.9 NETWORKING AND OTHER SOURCES OF HELP

There are many sources of help in the public and private sector which new museums might make use of at different stages of their development. Some provide advice in specialist areas of museum work e.g. marketing, financial planning, design and display, conservation; some provide financial assistance towards new developments; and some provide support and guidance on professional matters.

It is critically important to seek help and guidance at an early stage if you are lacking the professional skills or relevant information at first hand. Duplication of effort can be time-wasting and often expensive, and too often groups setting up and managing new museums fall into the trap of trying to reinvent the wheel when a little time discussing plans and needs with others, or reading relevant published material, could prevent later difficulties.

Area Museum Councils should be a first contact point for those setting up and managing new museums. The Area Museum Council's staff will be able to identify relevant literature, appropriate organisations and contact names and addresses at national, regional and local level. Section 6.0 lists a range of other useful organisations with their addresses and telephone numbers. A particularly useful reference book for all museums is the Museums Association's Yearbook which provides a wealth of information of direct relevance to museum work, contact names and addresses for museums and museum support organisations, and includes professional codes of conduct for museum staff and governing bodies, and committee members.

All of those setting up and managing new museums should recognise that they are entering a field where there is a vast range of professional expertise and experience. Making effective use of that experience in developing a new museum is a responsibility for all of those engaged with the museum. Sharing one's own experience with others is also important and those managing new museums should make every effort to work in partnership with others in the field and participate in professional activities.

## 1.10 LEGAL STATUS

A new museum's legal status is of vital concern and should be

> It is critically important to seek help and guidance at an early stage if you are lacking the professional skills or relevant information at first hand.

considered with the help of qualified legal advisers at an early stage in the development of a new museum. The museum's organisers will need to examine the most appropriate form of legal protection for the museum's collections for which they have responsibility (e.g. legal ownership, loan agreements, safeguards against dispersal in the event of dissolution etc.) and for themselves (e.g. personal liability of debts incurred, liability for injuries to visitors or staff etc.)

Area Museum Councils can provide general advice in this area with reference to the requirements of the Museums and Galleries Commission's national Museum Registration scheme.

Although there are other forms of legal status for independent museums, it is generally agreed that one of the most suitable forms for a new independent museum to have is that of a company limited by guarantee with no share capital registered as a charity. For smaller museums, company status may not be deemed necessary, but for larger museums it is generally recommended.

There are various advantages in having charitable status which will have a significant bearing on the working and development of a new museum. In terms of its collections, the status of a charitable trust provides the museum with safeguards against the dispersal or sale of items in the event of dissolution. It also protects the interests of donors who will have presented material to the museum on the understanding that it will be cared for in perpetuity.

In terms of a new museum's organisers, the constitution of a charitable trust provides a set of rules which acts as a legal framework for the museum's management. Incorporation as a company limited by guarantee normally limits the liability of the Trustees to a nominal sum in the event of insolvency, providing there is no negligence of Trustee duties. Rate relief on the museum's building(s) can also be claimed given charitable status.

Charitable status is also important in terms of fund-raising. It is a standard condition of receiving grant-aid from organisations such as the Area Museum Councils and the Museums and Galleries Commission. It is also an important consideration in approaching other potential financial supporters in the public and private sectors. Legal status of this type not only gives protection in law for the museum's

A new museum's legal status should be considered with the help of qualified legal advisers at an early stage in development.

c

collections and its organisers, but also provides increased credibility for the museum's work.

To provide detailed guidance on the drafting or amendment of a Trust Deed or the memorandum and articles of association of a company limited by guarantee, the Association of Independent Museums has prepared a range of guidelines on charitable status for museums. These include guidelines specific to museums in Scotland where the legal and organisational position differs to that of the rest of the UK. The guidelines cover such matters as the formation of companies, Trust deeds, duties of Charity Trustees, and the taxation of charities and covenants. They also provide specimen forms of a Declaration of Trust, and a memorandum and articles of association for a Company limited by guarantee with no share capital for drafting purposes. In England, the Charity Commission also provides published guidance om museums and charity legislation.

As legal status is an important component of Museum Registration, reference to the guidelines for Museum Registration is advised. Area Museum Councils are available to discuss new constitutions or the suitability of existing constitutions for Museum Registration purposes. You are however advised to seek independent and professional legal advice on all of these matters. The formulation of a suitable constitution for a new museum requires appropriate guidance from your solicitors.

### 1.11 POLICY DEVELOPMENT

We noted in section 1.5 that a museum should have a clear statement of *mission* or purpose. The museum can then develop a set of *key functional objectives* which provide depth to the mission statement. These functional objectives essentially demonstrate the museum's main objectives in the various fields in which it is working (see section 1.12).

The museum must also develop a set of *policies* relating to the mission statement and functional objectives which provides a framework for its activities. This is a key task of the museum's governing body. It is from the mission statement, functional objectives and policies that the museum is able to construct its forward plan which we discuss below (see section 1.12).

Policy development is needed in three areas - *collections management, public services,* and *museum management* - and is regularly referred to in sections 2.0 - 4.0 of this book. Some museums produce an integrated collections management policy covering such areas as acquisition and disposal, including loans, (a basic requirement for Museum Registration), documentation, conservation and storage, security, and disaster planning; others will have separate policies in each of these areas. Under public services, the museum will need to develop a communications policy or policies covering education, both formal and informal, interpretation, customer care and access, equal opportunities and public relations and marketing. Policies in the area of museum management include staffing and staff development, equal opportunities, financial, buildings management and maintenance.

The value of establishing policy statements is that they can be used as a basis for action, they are a constant point of reference for all involved with the museum, and they help to ensure consistency of approach. The process of developing policy statements is a discipline which helps to focus thinking on the part of staff and governing bodies. They should reflect or include statements accepted by the Museums Association and Museums and Galleries Commission in their various codes of practice.

The value of establishing policy statements is that they can be used as a basis for action, they are a constant point of reference for all involved with the museum, and they help to ensure consistency of approach.

Decisions taken by the governing body at its various meetings will cumulatively constitute the policy of the museum. It is the task of the museum's staff to recommend on policy matters and to implement that policy in practical ways. For example, a policy decision in the area of collections management might be to endorse a draft acquisition and disposal policy drawn up by the museum's Curator. This will thereafter be the rule or set of rules by which collecting is carried out.

In practical terms, it is useful to develop a policy manual for the museum which includes the museum's individual policies. The manual should list the governing body's decisions under the main areas of the museum's work, together with the dates on which they were taken. Reference back to the minutes of the meetings at which decisions were made can then be made if necessary for further information. This can then serve as the overall policy framework within which the museum is working and a useful reference for members of the governing body and staff. The manual should be reviewed on a regular basis and policies revised as appropriate in the light of change and development.

## 1.12 FORWARD PLANNING

Museums grow and develop; they face change in the context within which they are working at local, regional, national and international level and within themselves. At the same time they must maintain their services to the public and care for their collections in effective ways. Successful museums of all types and sizes recognise the importance of forward planning in helping to manage change and development. Forward planning shows both internally to staff and governing body, and externally to funding bodies, other supporters and the museum's users that the museum has a clear sense of purpose and a clear sense of direction. A forward plan helps to define the museum's mission or purpose and values, explains its functional objectives and policies, outlines its current position and markets, details its planning objectives and shows how these will be achieved through its available resources. The process of forward planning also provides a basis for assessing the museum's strengths and weaknesses and reviewing its performance and achievements.

A forward plan thus provides a sense of purpose and direction, inspires confidence in those who support the museum, and enables a museum to monitor its progress. Increasingly, forward plans are a requirement for funding bodies whether these be local authorities, sponsors, charitable trusts and national or regional funding agencies such as the Area Museum Councils or Regional Arts Boards. The Museums and Galleries Commission recommends that all museums should acquire the habit of planning in their work and while a forward plan is not yet a formal requirement of Registration, every encouragement is given to museums to think about their work within a planning framework.

There is no set structure for a forward plan; indeed forward plans are variously described as management plans, business plans, development plans, strategic plans, corporate, or organisational plans. What they do have in common however is the need for museum managers to think through what they want to achieve over a set period of time with the resources at their disposal. Without a forward plan, a museum operates in an ad hoc way and can waste the resources at its disposal.

Forward planning is best thought of as taking place on a continuous basis. Once a plan has been structured, it can be rolled forward on an

Successful museums of all types and sizes recognise the importance of forward planning in helping to manage change and development.

annual basis so that the museum is always operating within the framework of the plan. An annual report, which reviews progress against the planning objectives for the year, provides a vehicle for promoting the achievements of the museum. The forward plan and the annual report should be seen together as part of the overall planning cycle.

In drawing up a forward plan, the following steps should be considered:

1. A review of the museum's current position

For new museums the planning steps below are likely to be being undertaken for the first time and will require detailed consideration by museum management and staff. Where a museum is rolling forward its plan on an annual basis, it will not always be necessary to review all of these headings each year. However, all of the headings should be considered on a regular basis so that the museum is up-to-date with its current position.

It may be necessary to work with specialist staff from outside the museum on a number of these headings in reviewing the strengths and weaknesses of the museum e.g. architects, conservators, documentation advisers, education advisers, Crime Prevention Officers, or consultants.

In reviewing a museum's operation systematically, it is valuable to compare your museum and its operation against available standards, and to examine what other museums and allied facilities are achieving. This can be done through desk research using published material, or through visits and interviews with staff in other institutions, or preferably a combination of both methods.

In reviewing a museum's operation systematically, it is valuable to compare your museum and its operation against available standards, and to examine what other museums and allied facilities are achieving.

Reviewing the museum's external relations with patrons, financial supporters, sponsors, professional agencies is of particular importance. Building up good working relations with external agencies is a key aspect of museum management and should be thoroughly considered.

The comments on different aspects of the museum's operation in sections 2.0 - 4.0 of this book will help to focus attention on the sort of questions to be asked in reviews of this type.

Planning steps:

| | | |
|---|---|---|
| 1.1 | Review of current purpose and mission |
| 1.2 | Review of current functional objectives |
| 1.3 | Review of current policies |
| 1.4 | A marketing review of users and non-users |
| 1.5 | Review of collections management practice |

        acquisitions, disposals, loans

        documentation and databases

        preventive conservation

        storage

        remedial conservation

        research

        collections security

1.6    Review of user services and customer care

        information

        displays

        education services

        outreach services

        temporary/touring exhibitions

        shop/sales points

        catering

        publications

        events and activities programmes

        public relations and marketing

        user facilities - cloakrooms, toilets,

1.7    Review of management procedures

        staffing structure

        Friends/volunteers

Governing Body membership/committee structure

external supporters/external relations

staff training/development

museum security

administrative procedures

communications systems

buildings - use of space

buildings - internal/external conditions

buildings - maintenance

finance - capital

finance - revenue

fundraising/sponsorship

income generation

performance measurement

standards.

2. Initial drafting of the forward plan

In structuring the forward plan, the headings below will give general guidance. The amount of detail needed will vary from one museum to another, but it is suggested that the plan should cover a three-year period and then be rolled forward annually. If a longer period - say 5 years - is chosen, the museum is likely to find that projected action in year 5 can not be defined in sufficient detail to make its inclusion worthwhile. There may however be certain actions which do need a longer timescale than three years and these will need to be flagged up appropriately.

The various sections of the plan at 2.6 - 2.8 should identify specific planning objectives in the light of available resources, put a timescale by which they should be achieved and explain how their outcomes will be measured in quantitative and qualitative terms as appropriate. The Museums Association has developed a useful range of performance measures for use in forward planning and performance review and these are published in the Association's Yearbook for reference purposes.

The museum's plan will be driven forward by its financial plan which is an integral part of the plan. Forward projections for income and expenditure for the three-year period will help museum managers to see what can be achieved with known resources and what can only be achieved with additional funding. It is essential to be realistic and not to base programmes of action on funding projections which can not practically be achieved. Cash-flow forecasts on a monthly/weekly basis can be an effective method of determining fluctuations in income and expenditure and help to strengthen the museum's financial projections.

It should be stressed that forward planning is a relatively simple and straightforward task, although it can be time-consuming. Its long-term benefits however outweigh any short-term commitment of time.

Planning steps:

| | |
|---|---|
| 2.1 | Mission statement/statement of purpose |
| 2.2 | Functional objectives |
| 2.3 | Summary statements of policies |
| 2.4 | Historical development of museum |
| 2.5 | The museum's market |
| 2.6. | Collections management - planning objectives (see headings above at 1.5) |
| 2.7 | User services - planning objectives (see headings above at 1.6) |
| 2.8 | Museum management - planning objectives (see headings above at 1.7) |
| 2.9 | Financial plan and fundraising requirements |
| 2.10 | Time-scales and targets |
| 2.11 | Performance measures |

It should be stressed that forward planning is a relatively simple and straightforward task, although it can be time-consuming.

3. Agreeing and implementing the forward plan

Once a draft has been prepared, or as drafts of the different sections of the forward plan are prepared, managers should discuss these with staff and reach agreement with the proposed plan of action. The plan can then be formally presented to staff, and be put to the museum's governing body for discussion and approval or modification.

It can be useful to prepare a brief resumé of the plan for use in discussion with outside organisations or support groups, and the museum should determine which organisations should be circulated with a copy for reference or information.

The next steps are for managers to decide how staff will structure their time to meet the planning objectives in the different sections. While this will have course played an important part in matching objectives to resources (see section 1.7), it will nonetheless now be important to define these more closely and establish targets for each member of staff on an individual or team basis to work to. Managers will then be in a position to monitor progress against the timescale laid down in the plan.

> It will be important to establish targets for each member of staff on an individual or team basis to work to.

Planning steps:

    3.1    Staff discussions

    3.2    Draft presentation

    3.3    Finalisation of text

    3.4    Presentation to governing body

    3.5.    Agreement with governing body

    3.6    Production of plan and resume

    3.7    Circulation

    3.8    Staff/team target-setting against objectives

    3.9    Monitoring of progress

4. Evaluating and rolling forward the plan

Progress on meeting the museum's planning objectives should be reported to the museum's governing body on a regular basis. At the end of the year, the museum should produce an annual report which outlines achievements and progress and reflects the work of the organisation over the year. This can be as elaborate or simple as is deemed necessary, but it will be a useful public relations tool in approaching outside bodies for support, help staff and volunteers to see progress, and serve as part of the historical record of the museum's work.

Before the start of the second year's work, the museum's forward plan needs to be rolled forward to take in a new third year's work and to update the identified planning objectives for the coming year in the light of the first year's work. The museum manager needs to carry out this process in reasonable time before the end of the year so that the governing body can agree the proposals and the plan can be rolled forward.

The rolling forward of the plan will cover the drafting stage at 2 above and the planning cycle begins again. It may also need to take into account ongoing or specially commissioned reviews outlined in stage 1.

In this way a museum is always operating within the context of a forward plan and the plan becomes a basic management tool.

Planning steps:

4.1     Reports on progress to governing body

4.2     Performance assessment

4.3     Annual report

4.4     Roll forward

4.5     Redrafting programme (see 2 above)

Detailed advice on drawing up a forward plan can be obtained from your Area Museum Council. Further advice is available through the publications and sources of information listed at sections 5.0 and 6.0. Some museums may find it helpful to engage consultants to work with their staff on the production of a forward plan. It is important however to commission consultants who have a clear understanding and proven experience of museum planning.

Finally, forward planning should not be seen as a constraint. It is a basis on which to build effective museums. It is not an end in itself, but a means towards an end - making the best of available resources to provide a high quality service to users and to manage collections efficiently.

Forward planning should not be seen as a constraint. It is a basis on which to build effective museums.

# 2 MANAGING THE COLLECTIONS

'What on earth are you supposed to do when somebody enthusiastically offers the museum a number of tourist souvenirs from the Far East or yet another "interesting old mangle", and you don't want to disappoint them?'

## 2.1 ACQUISITION AND DISPOSAL POLICIES

Every museum should develop a clear, written policy on the acquisition of items for its collections, and their disposal. Such a policy provides a statement of intent for the museum's governing body, staff and users, and serves as a general reference point for decision-making. An acquisition and disposal policy is a key requirement of the national Museum Registration scheme (see section 4.5), and guidelines and model policies have been developed by the Area Museum Councils to assist museums in drawing up policies. An acquisition and disposal policy must incorporate safeguards to ensure an appropriate degree of protection and public accountability for collections held in trust.

A museum's acquisition policy will in the first instance reflect the purpose of the museum, and provide a basis for developing the museum's collections. The policy will define how the collections should be built up e.g. by donation, field collecting, bequest, or purchase, and what areas or subjects e.g. social history, technology, applied arts, or natural history, should be covered. It will include a statement of the geographical area(s) within which field-collecting should take place and indicate the preferred areas or locations from which material will be accepted into the collections.

Close liaison with other museums working in the same areas is essential to avoid competition and duplication of effort and expense. In many cases, museums will be acquiring items for their collections from a discrete geographical area. On the other hand, subject-based museums, for example those based on an individual or particular industry, may be collecting much more widely. In these cases, an item relating to a specialist subject in one museum may relate to another museum's local history. The policy should therefore recognise these issues and make mention of possible overlap. A collecting policy should seek to avoid conflict between museums through acknowledgement of respective collecting areas.

If an item is offered to the museum and falls outside the scope of its collecting policy, it is thus possible to provide the would-be donor with a clear statement of why the item is not relevant to the museum's purpose. With a new museum developing its collections, this is of particular importance as a refusal to accept an item, without an objective statement of the reason behind the refusal can offend. In such

A museum's acquisition policy will in the first instance reflect the purpose of the museum, and provide a basis for developing the museum's collections.

circumstances, an explanation of the museum's acquisition policy and redirection to a museum where the item would be more appropriately housed may avert a public relations crisis.

New museums should *always* avoid blanket requests for items through the media or other publicity outlets. An avalanche of items which fall outside the museum's acquisition policy can often prove a severe embarrassment. Carefully worded requests, explaining the scope of the museum's collections and acquisition policy are always to be preferred.

Many museums find it helpful to their users to have a statement of the museum's acquisition and disposal policy displayed or available in the museum. This does not have to be the full policy statement, but a resumé will help users understand how the museum develops its collections and the reasons for this. It also provides an opportunity to explain how the museum relies on the generosity of its users in building up collections.

In summary, an acquisition policy will cover the following points:

1) Aims and objectives of the museum

2) Schedule for policy revision

3) General rules for collecting and legal constraints

4) Acquisition procedures, including loans

5) Collecting area, and liaison arrangements

The policy statement should be reviewed on a regular, 3-5 years, basis.

## Constraints

There are of course constraints on collecting which should be built into the museum's policy. One of the key considerations in whether or not to accept an item is whether the museum can provide adequate resources for the proper care of the item. Is there sufficient storage capacity of an appropriate standard to ensure its safe-keeping? Does it require specialist conservation attention not available in the museum? Can the museum afford the remedial conservation programme required for the item? Does the museum have sufficient staff time to record and document the item adequately? Does the item need specific insurance cover?

The decision to acquire an item must always include consideration of the associated costs and the ability of the museum to look after the item effectively.

Questions of this sort reflect the fact that every item coming into the museum's collections has a cost attached to it - costs of staff time, display and storage space, documentation materials, storage materials etc. The decision to acquire an item must always include consideration of the associated costs and the ability of the museum to look after the item effectively.

Apart from the museum's ability to provide adequate care for an item, there are other considerations. Do you have examples of this item already in the collection? Can you justify acquiring additional items of a similar type? Does the donor/seller have legal right to the item being offered? Has the item been illegally acquired through theft or in contravention of existing legislation here or abroad? Can the museum afford to purchase the item? Will it be necessary to raise funds specifically for its acquisition? Are there unacceptable conditions attached to a donation? Can the museum meet the security, environmental and insurance conditions of a loan?

Such questions will need to be answered. Your policy will provide the basis for you to make an informed and objective decision on whether or not to take an item into the collection. It will include both ethical and legal considerations of the type outlined above, and provide consistency of approach to the museum's work.

A written policy statement will provide the context within which detailed acquisition and documentation procedures can be put into action (see sections 2.3 and 2.4).

**Disposal**

The assumption underlying the establishment of a new museum is that the museum will hold its collections in trust for the public benefit. Indeed there is a strong presumption in law against the disposal of items in museum collections. Apart from legal and constitutional requirements, a museum can quickly destroy its credibility and suffer immense public relations damage if it disposes of items from donors. Preservation is a key functional purpose of museums and disposal can be an abnegation of trust placed in the museum by the public.

A museum can quickly destroy its credibility and suffer immense public relations damage if it disposes of items from donors.

However, from time to time, every museum finds it necessary to dispose of an item from the collection. In most cases the circumstances are uncontroversial and straightforward - the transfer of an item which would be better housed in another registered museum, the destruction of a badly damaged natural history specimen, or the rationalisation of duplicates. Such decisions can be difficult to take, but a body of good practice has been developed over the years which provides guidance on effective disposal procedures. Guidelines, which are based on the Museums Association's Code of Practice on this subject, are available from Area Museum Councils.

A museum's disposal policy should therefore dovetail with its acquisition policy. It should cover the following points:

1)      General principles relating to disposal

2)      Reasons for disposal

3)      Authority for disposal from governing body

4)      Disposal of purchases, gifts, and bequests

5)      Disposal procedure

6)      Disposal by destruction

7)      Procedure following disposal

There are a number of particular points of concern. The governing body of the museum must take responsibility for decisions about disposals. Such decisions should be taken with the advice of the museum's curator or curatorial adviser. Where disposal has been agreed by the governing body, any conditions on items which have been purchased with aid from a grant-aid body such as the National Heritage Memorial Fund, the MGC/V & A Grant Fund, the National Acquisitions Fund or other similar funding source must be met. Records of disposals must be kept. Any money received from the sale of an item to another museum should normally be transferred to the museum's purchase fund to acquire new items for the collections.

The museum's constitution or memorandum and articles of association will include clauses relating to the disposal of collections in the event of the museum's dissolution. A disposal policy should make reference to these. In the event of dissolution, provision should be made for either the entire collection and associated records to be gifted to a nominated registered museum - such a museum should have agreed in advance to be nominated and have a relevant acquisition policy; or held in trust pending the emergence of a viable alternative organisation.

D

Professional advice should be taken on disposal matters wherever necessary. Reference should be made to the acquisition and disposal policy statements in the Museums Association's Yearbook, and to the Museums and Galleries Commission's Guidelines for Museum Registration.

## 2.2 FIELDWORK, COLLECTING AND RESEARCH

The acquisition of items for your museum and the development of the collections are key aspects of the museum's work. Some of the different methods for acquiring items are described briefly here and in section 2.3. In this section, we look at the role of the museum in actively collecting material, together with its associated information, 'in the field'. All too many museums still rely heavily on 'passive collecting' - the collection of items offered to the museum - even though they have a policy on acquisitions. Active collecting and recording programmes need to take place on a project or programme basis to secure and document items for the future. This systematic approach to collecting, rather than ad hoc acquisition, is seen to be of increasing importance in all museum work.

If a museum is to contribute to the development of knowledge in the broadest sense, it will engage in fieldwork and collecting as part of carefully planned research programmes. Such programmes will seek to acquire items for the museum together with as much information as possible about the context in which they were made, used or found. In certain cases, the museum will collect information in the field to provide contextual information for its existing collections. This may be through oral history recording, video, film and photographic survey, measured drawings of buildings, ecological surveys, and so on.

There are of course constraints on what a museum can or should collect (see section 2.1). A wide range of legislation exists, at British and European level, to protect the cultural and natural heritage and environment. It is important to be conversant with the principal legislation governing cultural and natural heritage matters. The museum will inevitably face limits on its staff time and finance for fieldwork. The necessary skills may not be readily available. Other agencies or museums may be covering similar ground. It is the task of the museum's managers to take such constraints into account when planning research projects and devising collecting programmes as part of the museum's development work.

There are different approaches to fieldwork and the collecting of information and new items for the collections. Each discipline or area of museum work - for example, archaeology, natural history, social history, or applied arts - has developed its own working methods. In some cases, such as the survey, excavation and recording of an archaeological site, highly skilled and professionally trained people are required to supervise the work. The expertise to carry out such work may need to be contracted by the museum as part of a research programme organised under its aegis. It is important to seek professional advice in such areas.

On a more general level, skills such as oral history recording or photographic recording can be acquired more readily by museum staff through training. Such recording, linked to carefully defined collecting programmes in different aspects of local or social history, can be invaluable in providing background or contextual information as collections are developed.

The uses to which information and material gathered through fieldwork can be put are varied - exhibitions and displays, publications and media stories, lectures and audio-visual programmes, leisure learning programmes, database developments, and so on. Some of these are explored in more detail in section 3.

Systematic, planned research can also demonstrate to the museum's governing body, funding bodies and the public that a museum is an active, rather than a passive, institution. It is equally important that such an approach provides many opportunities for public involvement and participation in the research and collecting process. Opportunities to work in collaboration with other agencies and organisations in carrying out research and collecting programmes mean that the museum is able to extend its influence and enhance its standing. For example, museums working with such organisations as the Workers Educational Association or university extramural departments, the National Association of Decorative and Fine Arts Societies, ethnic minority organisations, or local special interest clubs and societies, can benefit from the synergy that this creates. Through this approach, the museum can often harness additional skills to aid it in securing new knowledge for all to share in.

> Systematic, planned research can demonstrate to the museum's governing body, funding bodies and the public that a museum is an active, rather than a passive, institution.

## 2.3 DONATIONS, PURCHASES AND LOANS

Together with planned and systematic collecting programmes (see section 2.2), a museum will develop its collections through donations, purchases and loans.

### Donations

The majority of items in a museum's collections are normally acquired through donation by the museum's users. Donations to the museum may well be encouraged during fieldwork or as part of a systematic collecting programme. A museum's users often donate material as a tangible demonstration of their support for its work. It follows that the working relationships which a museum has with its users are important in encouraging such support.

Donations can arrive with little previous warning either through the 'front door' or through bequests. Wherever possible, it is advisable to discuss the item with a prospective donor or his/her legal advisers in advance of a formal offer.

Acceptance of items will depend on the museum's collecting policy and interests (see section 2.1), as well as practical considerations or constraints - size, condition, existing items of a similar type, legal ownership, availability of associated information, and perhaps value. The documentation procedures associated with donations are described in section 2.4. It is important to stress here that all donations, purchases and loans to and from the museum, should be carefully documented using agreed procedures. Without adequate documentation, it can be extremely difficult to establish legal title to an item in case of any later dispute over ownership.

Most museums make a point of using new donations for public relations purposes, to encourage further donations, to show their thanks to the donor and to provide publicity for the museum. Special exhibitions, press releases, a certificate recording the gift for the donor, or an information sheet discussing the item(s) donated, all help to create interest and to record the donor's generosity. Many museums will find that items are donated by individuals over an extended period of time. It is thus important to ensure that each item, whatever its value to the museum, is duly acknowledged.

*Most museums make a point of using new donations for public relations purposes, to encourage further donations, to show their thanks to the donor and to provide publicity for the museum.*

## Purchases

The establishment of a purchase fund provides the museum with the wherewithal to acquire items on the open market, through sales or other private arrangements. A special purchase fund allows the museum to move quickly if an item comes up for sale. It may however be possible to launch an appeal or seek a sponsor or patron to help the museum acquire an item. Much depends on the timescale within which the museum is working and the overall cost of the item. There are many case studies available to provide guidance on fundraising for purchases. Museums have a number of sources of financial support to which they can turn when an item becomes available for purchase.

The Museums and Galleries Commission has responsibility for two purchase grant funds administered by the Victoria and Albert Museum and the Science Museum in London. The MGC/V & A Fund assists museums, galleries, libraries and record offices in England and Wales not funded by central government, with acquisitions relating to the arts, literature and history. The Fund has some £1.5 million each year to distribute and grants do not exceed 50% of the purchase price. Grants are made on a weekly or monthly basis, depending on size.

The Science Museum Grant-in-aid Fund provides financial support to non-national museums in England and Wales for the acquisition and conservation of technological and scientific material, including natural history and geological specimens, and related archival material. The Fund provides financial support towards the purchase, transport, restoration and reassembly of items. As with the Victoria and Albert Fund grants do not exceed 50%. The Fund disburses some £0.25m per year.

In Scotland, the National Fund for Acquisitions is administered by the National Museums of Scotland in two parts, the Art Fund and the Science Fund. It contributes towards the acquisition of objects by museums and galleries, libraries and similar institutions. The Art Fund helps towards the purchase of items relating to the arts, literature and history. The Science Fund assists the acquisition of material relating to science, technology and industry. Grants towards dismantling, transport and reassembly connected with the acquisition process are made. The National Fund for Acquisitions provides some £0.25m per year.

> The establishment of a purchase fund provides the museum with the wherewithal to acquire items on the open market, through sales or other private arrangements.

These are important and well used Funds, and have been instrumental in helping museums throughout the UK in saving items for the public benefit. Their administrators are experienced in moving quickly to assist museums when items come up for sale at short notice. There are of course set criteria and conditions laid down by the Funds' administrators for grant support, and these must be adhered to.

Other Funds available to help purchase include the National Heritage Memorial Fund (NHMF), which has powers to provide financial support towards the acquisition, maintenance and preservation of land, buildings, works of art and other objects, of outstanding interest and importance to the national heritage. Any non-profit-making body one of whose main purposes is in the conservation of the national heritage, may apply for assistance. There is no limit either by amount or by percentage of the total cost of an item which the Trustees may give to a project. Grants have been given towards the acquisition of items ranging from works of art to scientific, industrial objects, and urgent and essential conservation work. The Fund does not give help towards a museum's running costs.

The National Art Collections Fund (NACF), which is a membership organisation, helps museums and galleries to buy works of art which they could not otherwise afford. It has made an immense contribution to the work of museums since it was founded in 1903.

In many cases these Funds work together to help museums acquire important items for their collections. Advice on funds available for the purchase of items for collections can be sought from Area Museum Councils.

## Loans

If the museum accepts a loan from whatever source, for example, a private individual, a national museum, or a public institution, it will need to provide appropriate documentation, insurance, security and preventive conservation safeguards.

It is generally agreed that a museum should give careful consideration to accepting long-term loans. Although the long-term loan of an item may have advantages in providing the museum with a unique exhibit or an otherwise unobtainable example, there are disadvantages. If the museum accepts a loan from whatever source, for example, a private individual, a national museum, or a public institution, it will need to provide appropriate documentation, insurance, security and preventive conservation safeguards.

The conditions placed on the loan should be clearly specified and the length of time for the loan should be agreed. Some conditions which a lender may wish to place on a loan, for example, permanent display, may be unacceptable, and negotiation will need to take place to allow for a compromise to be reached which is acceptable to both parties. If you accept a loan, you are responsible for it while it is in your care, and this may include responsibility for it while it is in transit to and from the museum.

There are a number of useful guidelines produced by the Association of Independent Museums and other advisory bodies, relating to this subject which cover in greater detail a number of the points raised above.

## 2.4 LOOKING AFTER MUSEUM COLLECTIONS

One of the primary responsibilities of any museum is the care of its collections. Care may take many forms - sound, well maintained buildings; correct environmental conditions in display, storage and working areas; appropriate storage facilities for different categories of items; avoidance of pollutants; suitable security systems and procedures; clear documentation and recording procedures; correct approaches to handling collections; suitable packaging materials for storage or transit; insurance cover - all of these reflect the fundamental responsibilities of the museum and together form the basis of collections management policies and procedures which all museums should have. Sections 2.5 - 2.12 below examine a number of these requirements in more detail, and highlight some of the dangers to which collections can be exposed.

One of the primary responsibilities of any museum is the care of its collections.

Most museums house 'mixed collections', that is collections of items made from different materials. Preventive conservation strategies have to take this into account in providing and maintaining suitable environmental conditions. Different materials require different environmental conditions. Maintaining your buildings to a high standard is a critical step towards obtaining good indoor conditions. Storage facilities and display systems have to cater for a wide range of artefacts and/or natural history specimens. Your forward plan should provide the framework for developing and implementing such strategies.

The museum's staff need to be trained in understanding their responsibilities in the care of collections. Job descriptions need to be written which incorporate these responsibilities. Training should be provided in line with appropriate standards on all of these matters (see section 4.5), and museums should seek professional help and guidance from conservation experts, Crime Prevention Officers, or documentation specialists in these key areas of museum work.

## 2.5 DOCUMENTING THE COLLECTIONS

Without effective documentation, a museum collection becomes meaningless, and the investment of time and money put into a museum is wasted. It is essential to ensure that your collections are properly documented and recorded. Wherever possible an item should also have a photographic record for security and identification purposes (see section 2.6 below). Documentation of collections enhances and extends their value. The quality and extent of a museum's collections documentation is a key component of Museum Registration.

*Without effective documentation, a museum collection becomes meaningless, and the investment of time and money put into a museum is wasted.*

A museum should know at all times what items it is legally responsible for and where each item is located within the museum. Without all available associated information, any item acquired by the museum will be of restricted value in historical or ecological terms. Without adequate documentation, legal title to an item may well be disputed. Without suitable documentation and indexing, the museum will be unable to use the collections for display or rersearch purposes effectively. Without proper recording, the security of the collections held by the museum cannot be assured.

Standards of museum documentation have been rigorously defined, and all new museums should seek help with this area of their work to avoid reinventing the wheel. The Museum Documentation Association (MDA) for example has developed a comprehensive range of documentation materials and services to museums. It includes a wide range of manual record systems and compatible computer-based cataloguing and indexing facilities. These developments have been underway for a number of years during which time curators throughout the UK have been involved in the research and development work associated with them. Museum Documentation Association materials are widely used in museums of all type throughout the UK. Local applications based on the same basic principles and procedures have also been prepared by individual museums. Advice and training in the use of these materials is given in printed manuals and factsheets, correspondence with specialist staff, regional seminars and roadshows, and advisory visits to your museum.

Advice on the correct methods of physically marking and numbering items in the collections is also provided. This practical and vital necessity should be carried out using appropriate materials. Much damage can occur to items if the correct materials and approaches are not used.

As computers have become more widely available in recent years, museums have developed extensive experience in their application to collections documentation. The range of software which can be used off-the-shelf for documentation purposes has increased, and so too has specially prepared software for inventory, cataloguing and indexing purposes. The MDA's own MODES software used for inventory purposes is an example of the latter. Other museum documentation services, like those provided to Scottish museums by the National Museums of Scotland, have also developed basic software for documentation use in museums.

Computers provide far-reaching opportunities for developing a museum's documentation system. Every consideration should be given to investing in suitable hardware and software, but professional guidance is first needed in assessing needs and recommending on the most appropriate solution. Where computer consultants are employed, it is a good opportunity to assess the full range of a museum's computer requirements beyond documentation, for example in word-processing, accounting, stock control and information about users.

### Documentation Systems

A museum documentation system will include the following main components:-

*Entry documentation:* this requires an entry form which is used to record essential information and supporting details about all items entering the museum as enquiries for identification (see section 3.9), potential acquisitions and loans. A copy of the form is passed back to the depositor as a receipt, and further copies are used by the museum to keep track of the material while it is in its care.

*Acquisition documentation:* in the case of an acquisition through donation or bequest, the formal transfer of ownership from the donor to the museum should be confirmed on a transfer-of-title form. Two copies should be sent to the donor - one to be retained by him/her and the other to be signed and returned to the museum for its files.

A basic inventory record of all new acquisitions and long-term loans should also be noted in a strong, bound acquisitions register. Registers are available from the Museum Documentation Association and include a number of introductory pages and some 150 double-page spreads for entries. The register is a primary record af all new acquisitions entering the collections. It records the unique identity number of an individual item or group of items, and provides a brief description suitable for basic collections management purposes. It also provides information about any disposals which take place from the collections. A second copy of the register should be kept in another location for security purposes.

*Item documentation:* when preparing a primary catalogue record for an item in a museum collection, full details about the item - whether an acquisition or a long-term loan - should be noted on a catalogue card.

Catalogue cards vary in level of detail from museum to museum. The MDA's specially designed catalogue cards for example are based on the same underlying philosophy and design principles as the rest of its documentation materials, and meet the special requirements of a particular subject. Each subject is supported by an instruction book which provides advice on how to fill in the cards. They include a general 'museum object' card which can be used for a range of objects, and the following:

Geology, Mineral specimen, Natural history, Archaeology, Ethnography/folk life, History artefact, Technology, Scientific instrument, Photograph, Military artefact, Pictorial representation, Fine art, Decorative art, Costume, and Numismatics.

In addition to these catalogue cards, there are also record cards which are used to provide a summary of any conservation work carried out on the item.

A museum's catalogue cards can be used as the basis for entries in printed catalogues of the museum's collections, for computerisation purposes, and for indexes to the collections. These indexes should include name, classification and donor indexes. The format of screen-based computerised inventory and catalogue systems can be designed to be compatible with card-based systems for ease of data-entry and for comparative purposes.

*Exit documentation:* items leaving the museum, for example, for exhibition purposes or remedial conservation treatment, should be logged on to an exit form. Copies can then be sent to the recipient institution or individual for acknowledgement of receipt, and also retained by the museum for control purposes.

A record should also be kept of the location and movement of items in the museum.

This work may seem at first time-consuming and a little complicated, but it is essential for the long-term safekeeping and identification of the collections. It forms a key requirement of Museum Registration (see section 4.5). Its importance should not be underestimated.

This work is essential for the long-term safekeeping and identification of the collections.

## 2.6 PHOTOGRAPHIC RECORDS AND COLLECTIONS

Photographs are used in museums for a variety of purposes; for example, for photo-documentation purposes, for contextual information for collections in displays, exhibitions and publications, and as archives. Film and video-film are also employed in many museums for display work and for recording purposes. Video-film is increasingly being used as a cheap method of photo-recording, combining as it does sound and moving pictures. Its long-term durability is however uncertain, and this may create difficulties for the future where permanent records are needed.

The first use of photographic recording is for the visual documentation of items in the museum's collections. Good quality, black and white/colour photographs should form an important and integral part of your documentation procedures. Items need to be photographed with due regard to their conservation requirements, and in such a way as to provide an appropriate level of detail. Record photographs should include scales wherever possible, and publication prints need to be of a high quality.

A comprehensive visual record of the museum's collections, whether on display or in store, should also be thought of as part of your security system. Without such a record, the recovery of items stolen from the museum becomes a great deal more difficult, if not impossible. Sets of photographs, particularly of complex objects, can also be invaluable for conservators if items are damaged or broken.

A second use is that of providing supporting or contextual information for the collections themselves. The ways in which items were made or used for example are often best presented or explained through photographic records. Such records may be produced through fieldwork in conjunction with collecting programmes, or collected specifically from a variety of sources, published and unpublished, to provide background information for collections of all types. Photographs and film provide a particularly powerful way of presenting natural history collections, as television has so well demonstrated.

Photographs may also be thought of as collections in their own right, where for example they demonstrate changing photographic processes or where they have been used specifically for artistic expression. Many museums develop collections of historic photographs of their areas or subjects, for instance, of street scenes, working life in fields, factories or offices, domestic scenes, buildings and so on. These archives can develop into important and often unique resources, and museums may be able to exploit them commercially through publications or framed editions, as well as using them as a primary research source.

Photographic records may be held as black and white and/or colour prints, slides, videos, films, inter-active video-discs, microfiche and microfilms. New forms of image-based information technologies are rapidly coming onto the market and their versatility and storage capacity should prove invaluable for museum purposes. New technologies, however, can be expensive and new museums should take professional advice with regard to their purchase and application.

Photographic collections of all types need to be documented effectively (see section 2.5), and stored in suitable conditions. Original prints acquired by the museum, or loaned to the museum for study purposes, should be copied so that negatives are then available for further prints to be made as required.

Appropriate conditions of temperature, relative humidity, light and air purity should be met when storing both negatives and prints. The type of storage materials used for photographic collections is also crucial for their long-term safe-keeping.

Equipment to take and/or process photographs can be expensive, and although many museums create their own darkroom facilities, it is advisable to weigh up carefully the comparative costs, as well as the time involved, between do-it-yourself and commercial work. The costs of photographic recording, whether carried out by museum staff or by a commercial photographer, should be fully understood and included in the museum's documentation budget.

Photographic collections of all types need to be documented effectively and stored in suitable conditions.

## 2.7 ORAL HISTORY AND AUDIO RECORDS

One of the most interesting and exciting developments in museum fieldwork in recent years has been the growth of interest in oral history and audio-recording. Museums have been quick to seize on the potential of this new approach for historical documentation and presentation. Planned programmes of recording personal reminiscences, life experiences, descriptions of working practices, and so on have given social historians working in museums a rich mine of unpublished information which museums have used in a range of different ways. Some of these include:

*     audio-illustrations for displays and exhibitions

*     audio-tapes on different aspects of local cultural life for study use

*     audio-tapes of personal histories reflecting change and continuity in the cultural and natural environment for study use

*     publications based on interviews on specific themes

*     tape-slide programmes for lectures and talks

*     resources for schools and leisure learning programmes

*     linked publications and audio-tape packs

The value of oral history is greatly enhanced if recordings are collected and transcribed on a systematic and planned basis. You may find it

The value of oral history is greatly enhanced if recordings are collected and transcribed on a systematic and planned basis.

helpful to collect material initially to support areas covered by the museum's collections and then extend coverage. In this way, discussion of items in the collections can help to support the information about collections which the museum holds and to bring collections on display alive. There are considerable opportunities for collaboration with other organisations such as community and adult education departments, and social services departments of local authorities, or other museums, and with support groups working for the museum (see section 4.7).

Reminiscence work with older people can have very positive benefits for the museum. Reminiscence work provides many benefits too for older people, helping to raise people's self-esteem and improving socialisation amongst the elderly. It can play a particularly important part in overcoming a sense of isolation in the elderly, and museums should make every effort to be involved in this area of work within the community. Reminiscence work, using kits or boxes of artefacts, photographs, video and audio tapes, should be discussed with specialists who care for the elderly. Such work may be less systematic than oral history programmes, and be more concerned with providing a service to a section of the community. Those who have passed retirement age do not traditionally use museums to the extent to which they might.

Whatever approach is taken, training in reminiscence work and oral history methods such as interview techniques and proper documentation procedures, and the use of good quality, reel-to-reel tape recorders, is recommended. It is important to gain permission from interviewees before their interviews are published or used in displays and exhibitions as recordings or transcriptions.

Audio records may of course not necessarily include the spoken word. Contemporary and historical recordings of factory machinery, street noise, steam engines, mechanical equipment and so on may all have a part to play in the museum, as may natural history recordings of animals and birds, and the natural elements. Audio records provide another dimension to museum displays and exhibitions, as well as study areas, and are a powerful and evocative medium which can greatly enhance a museum visit.

Museums engaging in oral history and other audio records need to consider how material is to be effectively stored, transcribed, catalogued and indexed, and how it will be cross-referenced to other records (see section 2.5).

## 2.8 PREVENTIVE CONSERVATION - LIGHT

Light can cause irreparable damage to museum objects whether these are man-made or natural. Light can fade colours and cause deterioration of the materials of which objects are made. It is often difficult to judge the degree of damage to an item which has been displayed or stored under adverse light conditions because damage can be such an insidious process. Any light, whether weak or strong, will cause damage: it is only a matter of degree. A strong light will produce approximately the same amount of damage in one year as a weak light, one tenth the strength, will produce in ten years.

Light intensity is measured in *lux units* using a light-meter, and all museums should own light-meters to test light levels on a regular basis. Recommended maximum values for light-sensitive materials range from 50-200 lux. The following values should not be exceeded:

> *50 lux:* costumes, textiles, tapestries, furniture, watercolours, prints and drawings, miniatures, postage stamps, manuscripts, wallpaper, dyed leather and many natural history and ethnographic items;

> *200 lux:* oil and tempera paintings, undyed leather, lacquer wood, horn, bone and ivory.

As a guide, an illumination value of 500 lux would be a 60-watt, tungsten, incandecsent bulb lighting the surface of an object at a distance of about 2 metres. You will appreciate therefore that when dealing with a museum display or exhibition it can be difficult to reduce the light level to 200 lux, let alone 50 lux: but it can, and must, be done otherwise the museum could destroy the object in its safekeeping. For a value of 50 lux, daylight is too variable, and light for displays of museum items will need to be artificially produced. Blinds should consequently be fitted to windows to cut out daylight where required.

Where artificial light is used, a warm-coloured light is preferable to a

Light can cause irreparable damage to museum objects whether these are man-made or natural.

cold-coloured light, which can produce a rather gloomy effect even at the same light intensity level. A combination of artificial and daylight sources provides the most visually acceptable results.

Light intensity should therefore be lowered to acceptable levels wherever possible. There are a number of measures which museums can use. They range from simple and cheap approaches to more sophisticated and more expensive measures. They include:

*Simple and cheap measures*

* moving items out of display cases near windows

* fitting curtains or blinds to display cases

* fitting manually controlled blinds on windows

* reducing the number and wattage of lightbulbs

* cutting out illumination when the museum is closed to the public

* fitting dimmer switches to room and display case lights

* blocking up windows

*More sophisticated measures*

* fitting time switches to display case lights

* fitting diffuser panels over lighting systems

* installing photocells in automatically controlled blinds

Apart from light intensity levels, the *ultra-violet* (UV) component of light is particularly damaging to museum objects. As ultraviolet radiation wavelengths are the shortest, they have the highest energy levels, making them particularly destructive. Daylight, and a number of artificial light sources, emit a high proportion of harmful UV radiation, the main exception being tungsten incandescent light sources. UV light should be eliminated by using UV- absorbing filters.

UV levels are measured by a UV monitor. Any measurement over 75 micro watts per lumen (uW/Lm) is considered excessive for light sensitive objects of the type listed above. The UV light source should therefore be screened by the use of laminated glass UV filters or acrylic or polycarbonate sheets; anti-UV varnishes or films applied to windows; and special filter-sleeves which slide over fluorescent tubes which emit UV radiation.

Without protection from excessive light, and its UV component, museum collections are at risk, whether on display, in store or in use. Every effort should therefore be taken to monitor light and UV levels on a regular basis, and appropriate preventive measures should be carried out where needed.

It is also important to explain to the museum user why these measures are being taken as visitors can sometimes be puzzled by low light levels in displays and exhibitions. All museums should make every effort to explain their conservation function to their users, and to engage their interest in how a museum meets its conservation responsibilities (see section 3.2).

## 2.9 PREVENTIVE CONSERVATION - RELATIVE HUMIDITY AND HEATING SYSTEMS

### Relative humidity

The environmental conditions under which museum objects are kept, on display or in storage, are crucial to their well-being. Of critical concern is relative humidity. Relative humidity (RH) is the ratio of water vapour in the air to the amount it could hold if fully saturated. Relative humidity levels are expressed as percentages. Thus low levels of RH imply dry conditions, whereas high values are recorded when the air is humid and unable to take up much more moisture.

Museums have thus to ensure that relative humidity is at an appropriate level for the material for which they are caring, and in particular they have to guard against changes in relative humidity. If the level of relative humidity fluctuates, it can result in the expansion and contraction of museum objects containing organic components, such as wood, textiles, paper, bone, ivory, or leather. Organic materials are also prone to attack from moulds and fungi when conditions are humid, that is over 65%. Metallic objects can suffer rapid corrosion and damage in similar conditions, and stone and mineral collections are also affected. Such change can thus cause irreparable damage to many different types of museum item.

Museums have to ensure that relative humidity is at an appropriate level for the material for which they are caring, and in particular they have to guard against changes in relative humidity.

The museum should aim for equilibrium conditions, with a constant level of relative humidity all year round. Relative humidity levels in museums should not rise above 60% or fall below 40%, and ideally, should be stabilised between these two figures. 50-55% is the commonly accepted compromise for a mixed collection covering a range of artefact types and natural history specimens. If necessary, micro-environments within these overall, environmental conditions can be created. Specially constructed display cases or storage containers, using silica gel, a moisture absorbing crystal, can be used to provide more controlled conditions for particular types of material.

Taking positive action to prevent conservation problems is known as *preventive conservation* (see section 2.4 above). Preventive measures of this type can avoid expensive remedial conservation where objects damaged by adverse conditions or poor handling have to be treated by specialist conservators.

### Temperature

Temperature is closely linked to relative humidity, since the ability of air to hold water vapour increases with rising temperature, and vice versa. Any changes in temperature, for example through faulty heating systems or climatic change, may cause the relative humidity levels in a display or storage area to move beyond acceptable limits. Objects placed close to radiant heat sources such as strong sunlight, spotlights or radiators, can also be damaged.

Museum collections do not require high levels of heating, and a temperature of 18°C (+/-2°) is a good temperature at which to aim for the display of mixed collections. Temperature levels in storage areas can be lower than those for visitor comfort. Provided that relative humidity levels are strictly controlled, temperature is adequate at about 15°C.

### Measuring relative humidity and temperature

Measuring conditions of temperature and relative humidity is best carried out by equipment which gives a continuous reading on a chart, and demonstrates levels and fluctuations over a period of time. The most common example is the recording thermohygrograph. Small dial hygrometers, showing levels of temperature and relative humidity, or simply relative humidity, can also be used in display cases and storage areas. It should be remembered however that these instruments do not record the environmental information, which must be checked and recorded by staff. Automatic sensing systems which can be linked to computerised recording systems are also now available. Advice on appropriate equipment to measure temperature and relative humidity in your museum should be sought from conservation specialists in your Area Museum Council.

### Heating systems and controls

Where temperature and relative humidity levels are prone to fluctuate, specialised equipment can be obtained to humidify or de-humidify display or storage areas as required. These are operated by automatic humidistat controls. However, a high priority should be afforded to installing a permanent, clean, heating system so that constant conditions can be maintained day and night throughout the year. Heating systems should be in the control of the museum. In buildings which are shared with other organisations, for example, museums can find that the heating system is controlled centrally or by another organisation without similar requirements to the museum. Under these circumstances, it is essential to have clearly defined agreements to ensure the museum's needs are properly met. Without a permanent system, dramatic and damaging fluctuations can occur with heating systems being turned off for example at weekends or in the spring and summer months.

> A high priority should be afforded to installing a permanent, clean, heating system so that constant conditions can be maintained day and night throughout the year.

Even where finance is restricted, some sort of control can be exercised through watchfulness and improvisation. For example, if a room is cold and damp, and it is warm and sunny outside, open the windows in daytime to let in some warm, dry air. Electrical heating is safe provided that the heating units are not positioned near to objects. Paraffin heaters, on the other hand, add moisture and harmful gases to the air and should never be used in a museum context. Commonsense precautions include keeping all objects off floor-level and away from walls (particularly external walls) where cold can cause water to condense. Allow objects space for free air-flow and adequate ventilation.

Conservation advice on controlling environmental conditions in storage and display areas, and for objects in transit, should be sought from your Area Museum Council or the Conservation Unit of the Museums and Galleries Commission. Your Area Museum Council will be able to advise not only on conditions and methods of monitoring and improvement, but also on sources of equipment and specialist services.

## 2.10 CONSERVATION - SOURCES OF HELP

As we have noted above in sections 2.4 - 2.9, there are two interrelated areas of conservation - *preventive* and *remedial*. The first deals with the conditions under which a museum item is kept in storage and transit or on display, and the steps which have to be taken to care for the long-term well-being of the item. The second is concerned with remedial work to an item which has been damaged through neglect or mishap. Caring for collections requires an understanding of their needs in conservation terms, and museums are able to draw on a wide range of support and advice, as well as training and information in this area from a variety of bodies. Some of the more important are listed below.

Caring for collections requires an understanding of their needs in conservation terms.

### Area Museum Councils

Area Museum Councils differ in the range of advice, support and training which they provide (see section 1.8). All, however, place a strong priority on conservation and are able to help their members meet their conservation planning objectives through practical support and financial help. They provide support to their members through conservation advisory services, environmental monitoring equipment loan schemes, publications and newsletters, information centres, manufacturers' and suppliers' databases and information, training programmes, discussion forums, and financial support and advice for implementing museums' forward plans.

A number of Area Museum Councils have specialist conservation services employing conservators to carry out remedial work on different categories of museum collections, on a rechargeable basis. Area Museum Councils also work closely with conservators in the private sector and in other museums, and can advise museums on the availability of conservators to carry out surveys of collections and buildings, or to undertake remedial conservation.

They work closely with the Conservation Unit of the Museums and

Galleries Commission and the Conservation Bureau of Historic Scotland.

### The Conservation Unit

The Conservation Unit of the Museums and Galleries Commission provides a comprehensive database of conservators working in England and Wales, the Conservation Register, and works closely with the Area Museum Council. It is matched in Scotland by a similar database covering conservators working in Scotland which is managed by Historic Scotland's Conservation Bureau. The Conservation Unit provides a range of advice for providers and users of conservation services, including guidelines in preventive conservation, and is able to award grants to help improve both conservators' skills and conservation facilities. It has an important networking role through its Conservation Register and is a key source of objective advice on selecting conservators to carry out work for museums. The Conservation Unit is also closely involved with developing standards for collections care in museums (see section 4.5), and plays an important part in European conservation networks.

### Other museums and conservation services

A number of museums, particularly the national museums and larger local authority museums and galleries, run their own conservation laboratories. In some cases, their staff can assist with advice and remedial conservation work for other museums. Some Area Museum Councils have agency agreements with laboratories of this type where the laboratory provides a certain number of hours per year for conservation work for an Area Museum Council's member museums.

There is a significant number of private sector conservators working in a wide range of disciplines. In some cases, specialist conservation is only available through this source; in other cases there are few private sector conservators working in a particular discipline. The Conservation Unit's Conservation Register, and its Scottish counterpart, will provide guidance on the availability of conservators to meet your needs and advise on the procedures for selecting a conservator and contractual arrangements. Area Museum Councils are able to provide financial support for work carried out both by their own conservators and those working in the private sector who meet agreed standards.

## 2.11 SECURITY - THE RISKS

National crime statistics continue to paint a depressing picture. In recent years, there has been a significant increase in recorded crime of all types. We have also seen often substantial increases in the value of museum material of all kinds and a wider public recognition of the commercial value of 'antiques' fuelled through the media. Thefts from museums and galleries, and other facilities such as historic houses and churches, are sadly on the rise, especially during public opening hours. To criminals, museums represent soft targets - they are invited in to look at items on display, and as visitors are often given a plan of the building and a list of its contents! There may even be the opportunity to observe and note security procedures and the location of security systems. Unless a museum is constantly on guard to protect itself, all such opportunities are used to the criminal's advantage.

Apart from theft, the increase in reported cases of criminal vandalism also gives concern. Vandalism can create considerable damage, which may be very expensive to repair. It may also disrupt the museum's procedures and affect staff morale. Vandalism increasingly includes theft and even arson. Civil unrest, which can include riots, bomb attacks, and disruption, both in city areas and in the countryside, has also become a concern for museums in different parts of the UK in recent years.

Crime therefore poses major problems for museums in all parts of the U. The museum has to face other risks - fire and flood perhaps being the most common. Some approaches and ideas as to how museums can counter security and other risks are given below. It cannot be emphasised enough, however, that all museums whatever their size and location, have to pay increasing attention to these difficulties and take appropriate precautions.

Crime poses major problems for museums in all parts of the UK.

## 2.12 SECURITY - THE SOLUTIONS

Drawing up and implementing security procedures and installing and maintaining security systems is a major responsibility of museum management. Where a new museum is being built or a building adapted for museum use, security safeguards should be included in briefs to architects and designers. Architects and designers should work closely with Crime Prevention Officers and security consultants to ensure that the museum can meet its responsibilities in this key area.

The special needs of museums have to be considered right at the outset of new developments, whether these be buildings, displays or exhibitions, transport vehicles or transit containers.

Some of the basic considerations and solutions are given below.

**Physical protection**

One of your front lines of defence is the museum structure itself. Strong physical protection should be provided to the shell of a building, with strong locks to doors and windows, skylights, cellar hatches and any other potential point of entry. Make sure that the doors and windows cannot be removed together with the locks! A door frame should be as strong as the door it supports. To supplement shell or perimeter security, the museum should also have internal locking systems which provide internal lines of defence. Other forms of internal defence are steel shutters or folding metal gates, and bars to windows.

It is important however that perimeter and internal security of this type does not conflict with fire safety measures, and guidance should be sought from Crime Prevention Officers and Fire Prevention Officers over any necessary compromise. Other points to note include securing upper storey windows and rooflights - these are often overlooked as potential points of entry; noting the location of adjacent buildings which might be used to gain access to the museum's premises; floodlighting the building for additional night-time security; and providing clear ground around the building free of potential aids to people intent on breaking in, such as lean-to sheds.

It is useful to carry out a security audit on the shell of your building and review security provision on a regular basis. Patterns of crime change and new approaches to defence against crime are developed over time. Your local Crime Prevention Officer will help in this work. The Museums and Galleries Commission's National Museums Security Adviser has developed security standards for museums and galleries and can provide advice on security matters on request to museums.

It is useful to carry out a security audit on the shell of your building and review security provision on a regular basis.

To support these forms of security safeguard, there is an increasingly wide range of alarm systems available on the market. Detecting a break-in can be achieved through inertia switches, vibration sensors, break-glass detectors and wiring within the face of internal doors. Alarm systems include those designed to detect movement inside the museum by passive infra-red, microwave or ultrasonic means, and by sonic means when areas of the museum are closed to the public. Emergency exit doors should also be alarmed to alert museum staff if a door has been opened.

In the daytime, or when the museum is open beyond normal opening hours, emergency buttons operating alarm systems, a coded message relayed over a tannoy system, a whistle or a hand-bell may all be used as a means of alarm. Alarms can consist of a bell or siren, and/or a remote signal linked to a communications centre operated by the alarm company, which will alert the police if the alarm is activated. Contrary to some expectations alarm systems do not catch would-be criminals! Their only use is to alert security personnel or police to danger. If the alarms are well designed, they may also give the police enough response time to catch the criminal in the act!

In selecting a security alarm system, first establish why you are installing a system and what you expect to get from it. You may have general needs, for example to meet insurance or indemnity requirements, or specific needs, for example to protect a single item. It is generally agreed that it is best to contract a national alarm company with local representatives to carry out installation and maintenance work for you. Such companies work to British Standards and have their own self-regulating watchdog authorities to ensure appropriate standards and after-sales service are maintained. Independent advice can be sought on your needs from your local Crime Prevention Officer, specialised security consultants, or in some cases, security officers of the national or larger local authority museums. Whatever system you choose, the museum will need to balance the costs of a security system against the risks being covered. Remember to review and maintain your security systems on a regular basis.

### Staffing

Apart from effective perimeter security, internal locking systems and alarms, there are other aspects of security to consider. Invigilation is a necessary component in your overall security strategy. The museum will need adequate staffing to cover the public areas of the museum by day. This includes cover at the control desk, in the display/information areas and in other public areas, such as gardens or toilets. Staff involved in security may also have responsibility for providing information to visitors about the museum and its collections. Where this is the case, it is important to balance these responsibilities to ensure that the security function is not compromised in any way. Such staff, whether voluntary or paid, should have clear job descriptions, regularly monitor the displays/exhibitions and other museum spaces, be trained to handle enquiries, know the museum's rules and regulations and the reasons for them, and know precisely how to react in the case of emergencies. Regular training programmes for all staff help to increase awareness of security risks and to improve understanding of security procedures.

Another component in your security strategy should include key discipline. It is often surprising how many people working in a museum hold keys which they do not require. Strict limits on the number of key holders and careful monitoring and checking of keys are very important, whatever the size of the museum. Spare keys should be locked in a secure key cabinet and keys should be signed in and out by a person responsible for their safekeeping.

The adequate documentation of collections is another security aid. This is especially true in keeping close track of the movement of objects, as well as in the recovery of stolen items (see section 2.5). Clear lines of responsibility for authorising all movement of objects in and out of the museum should be established. Any movement of museum objects places them at risk, from handling and transport, as well as loss and theft.

If an object is stolen from your museum, contact the police and the Area Museum Councils' Crime Reporting Network which will circulate details to other museums on your behalf. Your Area Museum Council is the point of contact. There are a number of specialised publications now available which will also circulate details of thefts of antiques and art objects to auction houses and dealers. Your Area Museum Council will be able to provide details of these and the necessary procedures to go through to include your details in them.

### Security communications

Internal, personal radio systems in larger buildings or on open air museums and sites are another device which security staff can use to keep in touch with one another, and report to a control point rapidly

Regular training programmes for all staff help to increase awareness of security risks and to improve understanding of security procedures.

in the event of a crisis. A number of systems are now widely and cheaply available on the market. Their use can also act as a useful deterrent.

Another security device increasingly used in museums to support security staffing is closed circuit television (CCTV). The saving of stafftime in installing CCTV is limited, and as a deterrent its value is more limited than some may like to believe. It is essentially only an extension of an attendant's eyes and needs to be used as such. However, recording video systems can provide confirmatory evidence of criminal activity and they can thus be useful in supplying evidence at a later date to police.

CCTV can be a particularly useful installation on doors as a security measure, and increasingly is being used for invigilation inside and outside museums to reduce security costs but maintain effectiveness. Infra-red television cameras can also be used to scan areas or perimeters at night. Where these are linked to computers, movement in the field scanned by the cameras will register automatically and alert security staff.

Museums should be aware of the costs of installation and maintenance of CCTV systems, and take appropriate advice on its use as part of their overall security strategy.

**Fire**

As with security alarm systems, automatic and manual fire alarm systems are designed to provide a warning to a fire station and to museum staff and visitors in order to elicit a rapid response. Automatic fire alarm systems detect fire, but do not prevent it! Your local Fire Prevention Officer will provide the museum with recommendations and advice over specific requirements under the relevant legislation covering the museum. One of his/her main considerations will be how to divide up the museum building into zones or compartments to contain a fire. A compromise may well have to be made in terms of the functional adaptation of buildings and design of displays to account for these requirements. Fire procedures need to be provided for all staff, who should be trained in their individual duties. Regular fire drill should be carried out so that everyone in the museum knows what steps to take in the event of fire.

Automatic fire fighting systems - water sprinklers or suppressive gas systems - are available for museum use; each has particular dangers, for museum collections on the one hand and people on the other. Modern sprinkler systems, however, can be zoned in areas of the museum which do not hold sensitive collections. It is worth remembering that the fire service can do more damage in putting out a fire which has taken hold of an area or building, than a sprinkler system can do in putting out a fire at an early stage!

Regular fire drill should be carried out so that everyone in the museum knows what steps to take in the event of fire.

### Disaster planning

All museums should have disaster plans for dealing with emergencies, for example, fire and flood, or bomb damage. Collections can suffer considerable damage after a fire or flood if correct handling procedures are not carefully followed through. Museums should draw up disaster plans which outline what and what not to do in the case of such problems, and what professional help to obtain. Regular training needs to be built into the disaster plan so that everyone knows in advance his/her tasks in helping to save the collections together with their documentation. An effective disaster plan can often mitigate the worst effects of a natural or human disaster.

### Vandalism

In dealing with the problems of vandalism, the museum should be aware of the virtues of good housekeeping and a friendly approach from staff. A well designed and presented environment is less likely to attract vandalism. If vandalism occurs, for example graffiti on walls or damage to labels, it is imperative to remove any signs at the earliest possible opportunity. Vandalism breeds more vandalism with inevitable, escalating consequences. It is also worth remembering that signs in and around the museum should be designed and constructed to resist vandalism. At the same time it pays not to appear aggressive or negative in the wording of signs. A friendly and polite request to refrain from a particular activity is much more likely to receive a positive response than a simple order not to do something.

An effective disaster plan can often mitigate the worst effects of a natural or human disaster.

### Security and success

In essence, museum security is made up of the following components - a strong perimeter shell to the museum building, supported by intruder and fire alarm systems, good key discipline, and well thought out and regularly reviewed security procedures such as baggage checks, visitor passes, patrol schedules for security staff and positive invigilation. Do not forget that it is not security staff alone who are

*All* staff are responsible for security.

responsible for security in the museum. *All* staff are responsible for security in ensuring procedures are rigorously complied with and proposals for improving security should be encouraged to be brought forward as appropriate. Training and discipline are the keys to successful security.

# 3 THE MUSEUM AND ITS USERS

*'Museums are for people, and the most successful museums are those which put their users first. The key to that success is putting yourself firmly and squarely in their position and asking what quality of service is my museum providing for its users.'*

## 3.1 THE MUSEUM USER

Museums vary significantly in the numbers of visitors they attract. Some may attract millions of visitors each year, while others may attract only a few hundred. In the United Kingdom, there are now some 100 million visits to museums every year - an indication of the very important role museums are now playing in the leisure and tourism market. Apart from visiting museums for exhibitions and displays, people make use of museums in a variety of different ways. They may not visit museums, but use them as a source of information for example. We examine below some of the services which museums can provide for their users. They include enquiry and identification services, research facilities, shops, publications, leisure learning programmes, and educational services. All of these are powerful methods of encouraging increased use of the museum both on-site and off-site. In setting up and managing a new museum, it is worthwhile investigating how other museums cater for different sections of their 'market' through the provision of such services.

Who are your museum's users? Visitor figures are clearly by themselves unsatisfactory in helping to build a detailed picture of a museum's visitors, although helpful for broad comparative purposes between museums. It is possible to obtain a general picture of the museum visitor from published statistical surveys such as Social Trends, or the General Household Survey carried out for central government or from published or unpublished market research. We know for example that visiting museums and art galleries is more common among people in non-manual rather than manual socio-economic groups, or that in general participation levels differ little between men and women. Detailed pictures are however more difficult to come by as market research often does not differentiate very closely between types of museums which can often be a significant factor in visitation. Certainly all museum audiences will contain a percentage of the 'average' museum visitor, but there are many factors in operation which will ensure that each museum audience has a unique profile or character. For example, physical location, type of collection, range of services, opening times, or size of building(s) are all factors which will affect the character and make-up of the museum's audience. Such factors may be out of the museum's hands, or the direct result of the museum's development planning and marketing activities.

The museum can use a variety of means to find out more about its visitors or users. In the first place, there is a wide range of published information on local, regional and national tourist and day-trip markets available through tourist boards at regional and national level. This information tends to be collected on a systematic basis and can provide valuable 'trend data' for museums to monitor continuity and change in these markets. Such desk research can provide valuable background information for more detailed surveys by the museum itself. In addition, it may be possible to obtain information about visitors to an area from detailed research carried out by other museums or visitor attractions. It is well worth spending time researching what published information does exist when building up a picture of the market(s) for the museum.

Secondly, there are now many market research consultants who can undertake market surveys of existing and potential visitors. While employing consultants can be expensive, the value of using professional consultants is that they use tried and tested methodologies to provide the museum with specific, objective data. They can also provide guidance in establishing systems in the museum for monitoring visitors and analysing the results to identify trends through time. For example, electronic tills in museums might be used to 'capture' a wide range of information about visitors, which can be analysed automatically; or museums might carry out phased surveys of visitors, which can be more or less detailed depending on resources, to help deepen understanding of what visitors enjoy most about their visit or what they dislike about the museum. Changes and improvements can then be made to facilities or services in the light of these responses.

Thirdly, there is the possibility of carrying out market research through collaborative surveys with other museums or visitor attractions in the same geographical area. Joint research programmes can help to reduce costs or provide more sophisticated data or analyses. It may be possible to secure grants for this type of joint research programme from economic development agencies, especially where a variety of organisations in an area are interested in analysing the visitor market such as museums, historic houses, hotels, restaurants, and garages.

The importance of understanding the market context in which the museum is operating, and the market(s) for the museum itself, cannot be emphasised enough.

The importance of understanding the market context in which the museum is operating, and the market(s) for the museum itself, cannot be emphasised enough. All museums in the UK work within a multi-cultural society, and must provide for multi-culturalism in their public services. Museums serve people, and as we near the end of the twentieth century, people's leisure time is increasing through shorter working hours and changing patterns of work. Museums are finding themselves in an increasingly competitive market-place. As a proportion of total consumer spending, leisure spending is on the increase. New patterns of leisure are emerging - leisure is increasingly home-based with a growing emphasis on new technologies, a greater interest in physically active leisure is developing, and people are now spending more time on themed holidays and special interest activities. There is a strong emphasis on good quality, value-for-money and high standards of customer service within the leisure and tourism industry. Such changing patterns of leisure time and leisure pursuits open up new opportunities for museums which are closely responsive to their markets, while at same time intensifying competition for capturing people's leisure time. Whether museums like it or not, their users will be subject to such market pressures and experience such changes in leisure activities. Museums therefore need to be one or more steps ahead in catering for these new market developments, while maintaining their unique role in providing their users with access to collections.

## 3.2 MARKETING AND PUBLIC RELATIONS

It is a common mistake to assume that marketing is synonymous with publicity. It is not. Marketing is the combination of methods by which a museum matches its different resources with the wants and needs of its users. Successful marketing in museums depends on people being aware of the museum's 'product' (its facilities and services), finding them conveniently available and deciding whether that product in terms of price and performance is able to satisfy their requirements. The relationship between the 'product', its price, its promotion, and its place or location, is known as the 'marketing mix'. It is balancing the interrelationship of these 4 'P's which is of crucial importance to the overall success of the museum.

## Market research

As we have noted above (section 3.1), a museum in the first instance must get to know its markets in detail. External information, published and unpublished, is available from a variety of sources - government agencies, local chambers of commerce, regional and national tourist boards, university marketing departments, other museums and visitor attractions - to help build up a picture of market size, and potential users. Internal information about users can be obtained from your own records, provided that these have been designed to give you the information you need.

Researching your markets, whether it is through using existing data or obtaining information direct from surveying existing and potential users, will give your museum a clear understanding of who your users are, why they visit your museum or make use of its services, and what their needs and expectations are. It will also help you to identify what sort of people do not at present come to the museum, and this will allow you to direct your marketing activities to develop new audiences for the future.

Market research, particularly the profile of users, needs to be a continuous exercise so that the marketing mix can be regularly reviewed and altered in whole or in part if required. This research will help the museum establish a marketing plan, so that the museum can be actively marketed and move forward in the market-place. The following description of the 4 'P's of the marketing mix will help the museum to develop a marketing plan.

> Market research needs to be a continuous exercise.

## Product

Museums are in competition with a host of other leisure attractions and activities in the market-place competing for people's time and money. Your success in managing a museum will depend how effectively you can defeat that wide-ranging competition by providing a 'product' - a mix of facilities and services - which provides better value and more drawing power than your rivals' products.

In setting up or managing a new museum, the quality of your museum and its range of services is a vital consideration. So too are the values which the museum stands for. Ask yourself what differentiates your museum from other museums and similar attractions? How does your

> In setting up or managing a new museum, the quality of your museum and its range of services is a vital consideration.

F

museum stand out in the market-place? Do you have a unique and recognisable identity? What can you offer that other museums and leisure attractions can not? The answers to such questions should help you to create a museum product which can compete effectively in the market-place.

The physical image which the museum projects is important in promoting the museum's identity. The quality of presentation and design of the museum and its facilities is relevant here. So too is the quality of the museum's print matter be it posters, leaflets, letter headings or newsletters. The style and presentation of copy will have an important part to play in this aspect of your work. It is well worth comparing the print presentation of a number of museums with the museums themselves, and asking whether the museum's print matter accurately reflects the character and personality of the museum.

## Price

Establishing a pricing policy for admission or services will to a large extent be determined by supply and demand. In a competitive market-place you will need to compare your own pricing policy to that of other museums or similar facilities such as historic houses. It will be important to work out what your users will be prepared to pay for the product you are providing. If the quality is high and the services are good, then you may well be able to set prices above the average. Your market research will provide guidance in this area. An imaginative pricing policy, giving due regard to concessions and designed to build repeat visitation, will help to encourage use of the museum (see section 3.4). Where an independent museum is receiving financial support from an external organisation such as a local authority, a government agency or a charitable trust, it may well be important to show that the museum's pricing policy is designed to cater for a variety of market segments. It is often helpful to explain the museum's pricing policy for users and patrons, and the ways in which income is spent, so that they understand how their support or patronage is helping the museum meet its objectives.

An imaginative pricing policy, giving due regard to concessions and designed to build repeat visitation, will help to encourage use of the museum.

## Place

The third element in the marketing mix is place or location. Place is an important factor in marketing. A museum may be located in one place, or may have a series of branches or outstations such as remote storage facilities. The location of a new museum will have to be promoted so that prospective users know where the museum is sited and how to get there. Marketing materials need to emphasise ease of access, provide simple to understand directions, and give an indication of the amount of time a visitor will have to spend using different methods of transport to get to the museum. A city centre museum adjacent to car parks, bus stations and railway stations, hotels, restaurants and shopping areas will have different marketing requirements to those of a museum in the countryside.

A museum situated in one place can however make its presence felt by providing a range of services beyond its four walls. Innumerable opportunities exist to deliver services outside the museum. For example, exhibitions can be mounted in a wide range of locations, such as agricultural shows, schools, hospitals, other museums, local hotels, or shops, all of which provide opportunities to display items from the museum's collections and help attract attention and support. Demonstrations, talks and activities programmes, or reminiscence programmes (see section 3.8) do not have to take place within the museum, but can be held in a variety of locations to encourage and reinforce public interest. Showing that the museum is actively engaging with its users in this way is a good method of promoting the museum, and helps to attract new audiences for its work.

Showing that the museum is actively engaging with its users is a good method of promoting the museum, and helps to attract new audiences for its work.

### Promotion

The last element in the marketing mix is promotion and publicity. There is a substantial amount of information available to museums in this area which reflects its crucial importance in securing interest in your museum. The first point in promoting your museum is to ensure that you devise methods of testing the impact of the promotion on your markets. If you have a limited budget to spend on publicity, you need to know whether you have spent it so as to get the best return. Surveys of your users will help you to gauge what form of publicity is most effective for the different segments of your market, be it paid advertising in the local press or on local radio or television, direct mail, or printed leaflets and posters distributed through outlets like tourist information centres or hotels. Ask for advice and support from regional and local tourist organisations, and examine other museums' experiences and obtain their advice. Explore whether there are any

A well thought through publicity programme, will help you reach into the market-place successfully.

grants available from your Area Museum Council or the Museums and Galleries Commission. Use your collections in different locations to attract interest in the museum, provided security and preventive conservation standards are acceptable, and your activities programme to help publicise and promote the museum.

Much good publicity can be obtained free through press releases to local newspapers or local radio stations which are hungry for local news. A good editorial or exhibition review in a local newspaper can be as useful for promotional purposes as a paid advertisement, even though you are not in control of the copy. Joint publicity programmes with other museums or associated facilities, for example through publicity leaflets covering museums in a particular area, have much to commend them. It is a good idea to plan a publicity and promotional programme through the year so that the museum is regularly in the public eye, and to develop close working relationships with journalists so that they can build up an understanding and sympathy for what the museum is seeking to achieve. A well thought through publicity programme, in whatever form it takes, will help you reach into the market-place successfully.

These four elements, the four 'Ps' of marketing - product, price, place and promotion - form the marketing mix. Getting the balance between them right is the challenge all new museums have to face. They should serve as the basis of a marketing plan for the museum. A marketing plan is perhaps the most cost-effective and constructive way of ensuring that the museum markets itself systematically, and a marketing plan setting out the museum's marketing objectives should be viewed as an integral part of the museum's forward plan (see section 1.12).

### Public relations

Good public relations are a vital component of effective marketing. They are essential to the success of your museum. Managing the relationships between the museum and the public on the one hand, and the museum and its funding partners or patrons on the other hand is a key task of management. If the relationship between the museum and its public is successful, then patrons are more willing to maintain and hopefully to increase their support. If that relationship breaks down or is damaged, then patronage and the investment or political support which goes with it can tend to dry up. Managing those relationships

Managing the relationships between the museum and the public on the one hand, and the museum and its funding partners or patrons on the other hand is a key task of management.

successfully is therefore all important for the well-being of your museum.

The most effective form of publicity is often word-of-mouth publicity. Good word-of-mouth publicity helps to build the reputation of the museum; bad word-of-mouth publicity can destroy it. In all your relations with patrons and users, direct and indirect, through the quality of your museum displays, facilities and services, the courtesy and helpfulness of your staff in answering questions and enquiries, or the corporate image of your museum projected through publicity materials or letterheads, you should seek to build up a positive picture of your museum. Museums exist for people, and in starting up and managing a new museum, your success will ultimately depend on the people for whom you are in business and who support your work.

> Good word-of-mouth publicity helps to build the reputation of the museum; bad word-of-mouth publicity can destroy it.

## 3.3 LOOKING AFTER YOUR USERS

The most successful museums are those which put their users first. A satisfied user provides the best form of publicity for your museum, and a museum should therefore regularly and systematically consider its overall relationship to its users in terms of the services and facilities which it offers them. No matter what the size and type of museum audience, the degree of thought which has been given to the comfort and convenience of users will always be apparent. Let's take some simple examples.

> No matter what the size and type of museum audience, the degree of thought which has been given to the comfort and convenience of users will always be apparent.

Have you provided visitors to the museum with somewhere comfortable to sit down and rest? Are there special facilities for disabled people? Do the museum staff know enough about the museum's services and collections to offer help to visitors if required? What consideration has been given to children's needs or nursing mothers? Can you provide cloakrooms and toilets? Does the museum have refreshments for sale? Can visitors buy publications, or souvenirs? Is the museum kept clean and tidy? Is it open when people want to visit it?

Some readers will undoubtedly say to themselves that they have neither the space nor the resources to provide particular facilities or services for their users. This may well be the case, but is there anything stopping you from producing a map or a leaflet explaining where the nearest restaurants/hotels/pubs are, or the nearest car or coach park? Even if you cannot provide a particular facility or service such a gesture will at least show you have put yourself in the position of the visitor and come up with a helpful answer. You will doubtless be asked questions about basic facilities again and again, and this sort of practical response will save time for the future.

Above all else the museum should strive to ensure that as many of its visitors as possible will come back - time and time again - because they enjoy themselves. Caring for your visitors and users is as important as caring for your collections.

The key to success is putting yourself in the role of the visitor or user.

The key to success is putting yourself in the role of the visitor or user, and examining the overall package or product which you are offering. Looking after your users, whether they are families or the interested individual, coach-parties or school classes, scholars or students, the infirm or the disabled, is one of the many responsibilities which go with managing new museums (see section 3.2). If you do not care sufficiently for their needs or wants, and if you do not trouble to find out what these are, your museum will soon suffer.

## 3.4 OPENING HOURS AND ADMISSION CHARGES

### Opening hours

The variety of opening hours amongst museums can be quite astonishing at first sight. There are no hard and fast rules as to when a museum should be open or closed. In starting up and managing a new museum, it is useful to examine the opening hours of other museums, historic houses and other tourist facilities in your area, and elsewhere, to help establish general guidelines for your own museum. Your opening hours will of course vary depending on your location, visitation patterns and the range of facilities and services which you have on offer. Seasonal changes in visitation patterns may well mean that your museum is likely to attract more visitors in the summer months than in the late autumn or winter. The summer holiday season and longer daylight hours mean a greater movement of people intent on leisure activities. There may well be other 'peaks' in visitor numbers at other times of the year such as Easter, Christmas, or bank holidays. Museums should take the opportunity to capitalise on such seasonal increases, through for example evening opening, as long as resources can sustain the additional staffing and running costs which will need to be met.

Active marketing of the museum will gradually increase your visitor numbers overall, although there may be a point beyond which it is neither possible, nor perhaps desirable, to go. Your museum may not be able to deal physically with increased numbers of visitors, or there may be good conservation reasons for restricting numbers. You may not want to sacrifice quality for quantity. You may wish to put greater effort into encouraging increased use of the museum by the local community at those times of the year when the tourist season is over or not yet begun. Opening hours and appropriate pricing would therefore need to be used as part of your marketing strategy.

Opening hours will often have to be decided some considerable time in advance in order for them to be included in tourist literature and promotional leaflets. Do make sure that you stick by published opening times. Nothing is more annoying for the potential visitor to read a museum's opening hours on publicity material, then to arrive at the museum and to find it closed when it should by all accounts be open! The effort a family may have made to get to your museum in terms of planning and travel time there and back, is essentially a gesture of good faith. There may also be significant costs associated with the trip. If access is denied, the results can be individually or cumulatively very damaging in public relations terms. If for reasons beyond your control the museum has to close, do apologise to disappointed users through appropriate notices and a message on the telephone-answering machine explaining when the museum can next be visited and what events are planned. Such consideration is simply a matter of good manners and can help to allay disappointment.

Opening hours and appropriate pricing need to be used as part of your marketing strategy.

## Admission charges

Like opening hours, admission charges whether they are levied on a compulsory or voluntary basis, vary greatly from museum to museum. It is well worth exploring what other institutions are charging their visitors in your area before fixing on a scale of admission charges. More and more museums are gearing their admission charges to different segments of their market and charging different rates for family tickets, local season tickets, tickets for the unemployed, senior citizens, children, or coach parties. Such a pricing range can demonstrate that the museum is concerned about its users' ability to pay for admission, as well as encouraging people into the museum who might otherwise not visit on the basis of one set admission charge. Your revenue income estimates and cash-flow forecasts will need however to take such a pricing policy firmly into account.

Whatever pricing policy is established, ensure that your visitors feel that they are getting value-for-money. The duration of a visit and the range of activities for visitors to engage in are important factors here. The longer a visitor stays in the museum the more opportunity there is to increase catering and retail sales. The level of admission charges should be set so as to encourage sales or voluntary donations in other parts of the museum.

One point to bear in mind when designing a pricing policy is that the point of sale for admissions is an excellent opportunity for promotion and publicity. Four pink cloakroom tickets in exchange for say £6.00 from a family of four who have travelled thirty miles especially to get to your museum are unlikely to impress! A friendly welcome, a well designed ticket showing how the museum spends its income together with a family souvenir leaflet, a plan of the museum, a children's leaflet, and a leaflet explaining the museum's forward planning and describing the Friends' annual events programme, for example, give the visitors the feeling you are interested in them. The return to the museum is good word-of-mouth publicity, publicity material which the visitor is less likely to discard at the end of the visit, and in the long term, increased support and repeat visitation.

## 3.5 DISPLAYS

In museum work, the term 'displays' implies some degree of permanence. The term 'permanent displays' implies fossilisation and should be avoided at all costs! Displays form part of the museum's overall communications system with its users. Other elements can include for example, exhibitions, publications, education services, leisure learning programmes, marketing materials and enquiry desks. In developing a new museum, it is helpful to establish a communications policy and plan for the museum so that it is clear what you want to say to your users and what media you will use to impart

Whatever pricing policy is established, ensure that your visitors feel that they are getting value-for-money.

In developing a new museum, it is helpful to establish a communications policy and plan for the museum so that it is clear what you want to say to your users and what media you will use to impart information to them.

information to them. Such a communications plan should form part of your overall forward plan for the museum and will indicate how your resources can be most effectively deployed to support your communications policy. Museum displays are likely to form an important component in your communications planning.

Their relationship to temporary exhibitions, and to events and activities, is an important consideration in thinking about displays (see section 3.5). A growing number of museums have decreased the amount of space available for displays, and given more space over to temporary exhibitions and activities space to provide a greater degree of change for their users. Change can then be actively marketed, especially to local communities, and the museum can avoid the accusation of 'always being the same'. This approach can have a sizeable influence on building up local constituencies of support for the new museum, and you may well find that in the early years of your museum's development such a policy is well worthwhile.

In planning displays for your museum, it is a major advantage to work with a professional museum designer from an early stage. This approach provides you with a range of specialist experience in project management, display techniques and preventive conservation, can save you considerable time in the long run, and provides a high quality presentation for your visitors. Museum visitors are becoming increasingly sophisticated in their level of expectation, and good quality design will help to meet that expectation. Museum displays do not need to be over-glossy, or 'high-tech'. They do however need to emphasise the 'real thing' which is the great strength of museums in comparison to visitor centres or heritage centres which are not collections-based and are often very unchanging. Supporting information, however it is presented, should not overpower original objects or specimens. It should help to provide a context within which original material fits and give insights into its production, use or life.

Some of the points to bear in mind when planning displays include:

* the relationship of your displays to other local or regional interpretive facilities and historic/natural sites

* research programmes to be carried out and the time needed for them to be undertaken

* collecting programmes to be carried out

* what information you want to give to your visitors

* the range of items - two- or three-dimensional - which you will want to include in the display and their availability and preventive/remedial conservation needs

* how to use the available space in display areas and display cases most efficiently

* the form(s) of lighting required - daylight and/or artificial - and conservation constraints

* text graphics - style, design, content, readability

* colours and textures

* illustrations - photographs, maps, diagrams etc.

* copyright requirements

* models and mannequins

* replicas and reproductions

* audio and audio-visual material and its presentation

* supporting information - publications, guidebooks, marketing materials

* information technology to be used

* special requirements for disabled visitors - induction loop systems, braille lettering, touch exhibits, height of texts

* security requirements

A good brief is the first step towards a successful display.

The list is a long one, and one of the benefits of using professional designers for display work is that their training and experience in the long-term saves time and money. A great deal can be learnt through working closely with professional designers provided that respective responsibilities are clearly defined and understood. This is the task of the brief. A good brief is the first step towards a successful display.

## Briefing

A designer will need in the first instance an outline brief from you to work to. An outline brief should include:

* the aim of the displays

* the space(s) to be used

* the target audience(s)

* details of the storyline or themes to be explored in the displays

* the choice of items from your collections to illustrate the themes, their size, and any special requirements for conservation and security

* choice of illustrative material including audio and audio-visual material to be included

* required time schedule

* proposed costs

* any other constraints or requirements

The outline brief provides the basis for the designer to discuss with you in detail the design solution and to produce sketch designs so that a preferred option can be chosen and worked up to a detailed design. Specification drawings, sub-contracting, production and installation will then follow.

The designer will not do your part of the work for you. As the design process progresses the designer will expect you to provide a detailed brief which will include full details, photographs and sizes of the two-dimensional and three-dimensional items for display, a range of illustrative material to support your selection of original material, completed texts and captions for descriptive purposes, and information on conservation schedules and requirements. It is not the designer's job to search for illustrations (although this can be sub-contracted to a specialist researcher), decide on the choice of items from the museum's collections for display, or produce information about the objects or research and write texts and captions for the storyline(s). It is the designer's job to weld all of these various elements into attractive and informative displays. Delays within an agreed time schedule can

Designing new displays should be a creative and enjoyable experience, although it will always be hard work!

cost money and it is thus vital to start out with a clear understanding of each other's role and responsibilities in the design and production of new displays. Designing new displays should be a creative and enjoyable experience, although it will always be hard work! Two aspects of display development are of particular importance for those starting up and managing new museums - writing texts and evaluation.

### Texts

In writing texts for displays it is best to use a professional copywriter wherever possible. Many museum texts are far too complicated and over-long because they tend to be written by specialists who know far more about their subject than the casual visitor. Museum text needs to be appropriately structured and highly readable and every effort should be made to keep text simple and short. The nature of a museum visit tends to mean that people are standing or walking while reading. Not only is this tiring, but it means that there is a limit to what people can take in. A good copywriter will present text in a form and layout which helps visitors assimilate information without overburdening them. The most successful museum texts tend to be written at four levels and presented in different type sizes - a title, an introductory statement of say one or two sentences, a descriptive passage providing more information in support of the introduction and captions for objects indicating their significance and giving relevant details. This allows visitors to read at different depths at different points in the display but nonetheless obtain an overview of the storyline through the titles and introductory texts to help contextualise the objects on display. The most successful museum displays tend to be clearly structured with an introduction, location maps, section divisions, and an ending rather like the structure of a story. Visitors often find a simple leaflet of the display and a basic description a valuable aid in orientating themselves.

A good copywriter will present text in a form and layout which helps visitors assimilate information without overburdening them.

### Evaluation

Evaluation is of increasing importance in museums. There are a number of different methods of evaluating displays and exhibitions in museums. The most common is a three-fold system known as *front-end evaluation, formative evaluation and summative evaluation. Front-end evaluation* is carried out before displays or exhibitions have been designed and is based on discussing with potential visitors in focus groups their interests and needs in terms of the display. The museum manager is here acting in an enabling or facilitating way and seeking to match the museum product to the needs of the museum's market. Feedback from this front-end evaluation process can be of enormous assistance in developing the brief for the displays and ultimately in maximising interest in them. A second strand in front-end evaluation is to discuss the aims and objectives of the display with other specialists and colleagues. Their guidance and assistance can help to enrich the value of the displays and ensure that the displays will be accurate and up-to-date.

*Formative evaluation* consists of testing the effectiveness of displays or exhibitions before the museum commits funding to a final design solution. Simple mock-ups of sections of display are developed and tested on a sample of visitors. Texts can be assessed in this way too. In formative evaluation you are enlisting the help of the people who will be experiencing the final results. Modifications and additions can be carried out in the light of their comments and reactions.

*Summative evaluation* is the evaluation of the finished displays. There is a variety of techniques involved in summative evaluation from the more sophisticated (video-recording of visitors' behaviour and specialist analysis) to the simple and straightforward (personal interviews with visitors). Whatever system is used, museums should evaluate displays and exhibitions so that they can demonstrate to funding bodies and patrons, as well as their public audiences, that they have been successful in carrying out their work and that the often significant investment made in new displays has been fully justified.

Museums should evaluate displays and exhibitions so that they can demonstrate that the often significant investment made in new displays has been fully justified.

## Working with designers

Information on professional museum designers and selection procedures can be obtained from your Area Museum Council. Care should be taken to select a designer with whom you feel you can have a good working relationship. Before appointing a designer from a short list of possible candidates, it is worthwhile talking to museum curators who have already used his or her services and looking at their results of their work in other museums. In particular, discuss with other museums how well the designer managed the overall project, how he or she responded to the brief, whether the overall quality of service was satisfactory and whether the budget was adhered to. Once you have selected the designer, ensure that there is a clear, written

Care should be taken to select a designer with whom you feel you can have a good working relationship.

agreement or contract which both parties sign, and which defines the designer's fees and expenses.

## 3.6 EXHIBITIONS

The two forms of temporary exhibition available to the museum are those which are created in-house by the museum and those which are brought in ready-made from outside. An active programme of temporary exhibitions forms part of the museum's communications plan (sees section 3.5). Temporary exhibitions, which may last for up to three months or so, serve the important purpose of creating visible change in the museum. As we have noted already (section 3.1) marketing change helps to create new audiences for the museum and to retain existing ones. In starting up and managing a new museum, the space available for displays and/or temporary exhibitions needs to be carefully analysed to ensure its most effective use. An increasing number of museums are integrating temporary exhibition space within display areas, so that core displays provide a context for regularly changing exhibits. This is an efficient use of space, creates change at low cost, allows reserve collections to be used more actively, and is less time-consuming than producing large scale exhibitions on a stand-alone basis.

You may wish to give special emphasis to temporary exhibitions to help target new segments of your local audience, and to encourage them to visit your museum on a regular rather than a once and for all basis. No cinema manager would expect to attract people to her cinema if she showed the same film every night and every afternoon for six months, a year or five years! Tourist visitors may perhaps come to the museum only once, but your local audience or the day-trip market in your catchment area can hardly be expected to attend regularly if there is little change in what to see or what to do.

Your local audience or the day-trip market in your catchment area can hardly be expected to attend regularly if there is little change in what to see or what to do.

Temporary exhibitions can be of a wide range of sizes and a wide variety of subjects. They can provide opportunities to display parts of your collections normally held in reserve because of lack of display space, to show what new items have been added to your collections, to highlight particular themes or subjects in your displays in greater depth, or to bring into the museum a range of material otherwise not available to the museum on a permanent basis. Even the smallest museum can accommodate some temporary exhibition space, either within display areas or in a separate area. The opportunity to display items from your collections off-site, perhaps in other museums or exhibition spaces, should also be examined.

A temporary exhibitions programme can allow community groups, or individual collectors, the opportunity to display their work or collections in the museum. This has the benefit of forging working relationships within the community, although care should be taken to ensure that exhibitions of this type do not impose constraints and restrictions on planning exhibition programmes. The museum must exercise a degree of quality control on temporary exhibitions brought in from outside the museum, and standards must be established to ensure the reputation of the museum is maintained.

In designing temporary exhibitions in-house, flexibility is the key requirement. You may wish to build up a stock of display cases and screens specifically for temporary exhibition use, and there are numerous ready made systems of this type on the market. These can however be expensive to buy, and provided that the materials have been tested for their suitability in terms of preventive conservation, you may find that it is cheaper to have display cases and screens produced locally to an appropriate design. A professional designer and a conservator can help with advice in this area. Your Area Museum Council will be able to assist with information about exhibition systems, and it is worth discussing the advantages and disadvantages of particular systems with colleagues in other museums.

Information about touring exhibitions, including costs and availability, can be obtained through the Area Museum Councils' touring exhibitions information circular. This lists ready-made exhibitions for hire throughout the UK. The use of touring exhibitions can provide greater variety for your temporary exhibitions programme and allow staff in your own museum more time to research and prepare in-house exhibitions. The planning and design of temporary exhibitions follows a similar pattern to the planning and design of displays (see section 3.5), although by their very nature should take less time to develop.

A temporary exhibitions programme should also serve as a focus for a range of events and activities or leisure learning programmes, and these may well include educational programmes (see sections 3.7 and 3.8).

A temporary exhibitions programme should serve as a focus for a range of events and activities or leisure learning programmes.

## 3.7 EDUCATION PROGRAMMES

Museums are first and foremost educational and scholarly institutions in the broadest sense. All museums should be considered as important resources for lifelong learning, and their collections and the information associated with them can be used for educational purposes for people of all ages, whether in organised groups or as individual students. In this section, we focus on children engaged in programmes of formal learning at primary and secondary school. Schoolchildren, particularly at primary and early secondary level, are likely to form an important sector of your museum's market. The majority of museums provide some sort of education service for their younger users. The form and extent of that service will vary depending on the museum's location, its collections and the staff and financial resources available, but every museum should draw up an educational policy and establish some form of educational service for schools.

Radical changes have been affecting the schools curriculum at primary and secondary level in all parts of the UK in recent years, and the consequences of those changes are progressively making themselves felt. Museums should have an increasingly important role to play in providing educational opportunities firmly in line with curricular requirements for children of all ages. Local or devolved management of schools in the local authority sector will continue to have an impact on the way museums organise and structure their educational services for some years to come. Museums will need to market themselves effectively to schools to ensure that there is take-up of their educational services whatever form these take. Some museums will concentrate their efforts on producing resource materials based on their collections for children and/or teachers, and making these available through appropriate channels. Others will go one step further and develop opportunities for direct contact between staff and children and/or teachers. The provision of an education service, however basic, will help to build support and understanding for the museum's work among your younger visitors. It will also help to ensure that visits to the museum are of real educational value, and not simply organised by the school for recreational purposes. The key point to remember in developing educational services for schools is that children should be brought into contact with the museum's collections at first hand. The production of resource materials can be very valuable in helping to contextualise collections, but should not be seen as a substitute for experiencing the collections themselves.

### Resource materials

The production of resource materials for your target audience(s) will require some initial investment of time and money. Support for this work may be forthcoming from local education authorities or it may be possible to produce materials in collaboration with a network of museums in your area or with museums holding collections of similar type. Once resource materials have been produced, they can be made available on a regular basis for all visiting groups or individuals. Resource materials of value to children might include worksheets, information sheets, children's guidebooks, postcards, replicas, or other publications developed in the museum or brought in from outside. Worksheets and information sheets should be prepared by professional teachers and be well designed and produced. They should encourage children to look at the museum's collections in detail and ask relevant questions about museum items.

Teachers welcome well designed information about the museum, its services and facilities, and its collections. It is also helpful to indicate how your collections might be used to underpin different aspects of the curriculum at primary and secondary level. Most local education authorities have a schools newsletter and these can often be used for distributing information about the museum, its services and current events and activities. A teachers' information pack can be developed for use in planning and preparing visits to the museum and should include practical suggestions as to how the museum and its collections can be used most effectively in their work. It follows that new museums need to make every effort to understand teachers' needs and objectives. Setting up an education advisory group or employing educational consultants to advise on educational policies and programmes can be a useful and practical first step in developing your educational service.

Some museums will have the staff time and resources available to provide direct contact with visiting school groups. Such a service might include talks in display and exhibition areas, illustrated lectures, handling sessions, drama or role play, or demonstrations. You may feel that limited time is more effectively spent on talking directly to teaching staff at in-service training sessions arranged by individual schools or

> Teachers welcome well designed information about the museum, its services and facilities, and its collections.

G

the local education authority. This approach can be helpful for a number of reasons. First, the teachers are the people best placed to teach their pupils in the museum and the classroom. Guidance given through in-service training can be built on for the future so that individual teachers become increasingly conversant with the museum and its collections. Secondly, in-service training allows museums to come into contact with a variety of subject specialists and alerts them to the opportunities the museum's collections provide for their particular subjects. Thirdly, in-service training can be especially helpful in developing networks of contact with teachers who may be prepared to help the museum on a voluntary basis and provide other informal educational activities, such as leisure learning programmes in the holidays or young people's museum clubs at weekends.

As we have already noted, a museum education service might also be developed to serve other groups. Adult and community education classes represent another important education market and the museum can provide valuable support here too. Where a museum is having to provide an education service to schools through a subscription scheme in order to cover costs, additional income from adult and community education sources, or reminiscence work may help to keep the service in being if its costs can not be wholly recovered through schools' subscriptions.

## 3.8 LEISURE LEARNING PROGRAMMES

An interesting programme of events and activities based on the museum's services can have a major impact on the public perception of your museum.

Your museum's displays and temporary exhibitions programme will attract visitors, but if they are complemented by lively leisure learning programmes much more value can be gained from your investment in them. An interesting programme of events and activities based on the museum's services can have a major impact on the public perception of your museum. Such a programme can be designed to develop new audiences by carefully targeting leisure learning programmes at different segments of your market and will foster interest in, and support for, the museum. A new museum has to work hard to build and maintain audience interest and leisure learning programmes are a powerful method of achieving this objective.

Leisure learning programmes need not be based only in the museum. Many small, new museums will not necessarily have space to run extensive activities programmes. However, there are many opportunities to run leisure learning programmes outside the museum in other locations, perhaps in conjunction with other organisations. Apart from their intrinsic interest for participants, leisure learning programmes can provide good publicity for the museum and encourage participation in the museum's work at all levels.

The following examples give an indication of possible leisure learning activities. In looking through them, consider how your museum might work with other organisations in carrying these out and how a planned programme of events and activities might be structured over the working year.

* object of the week/month, focusing special attention on items from the collections, a loan or a new acquisition

* video/film showings

* workshops for children

* family workshops

* print/picture loan schemes

* coffee mornings organised by your Friends' Group

* museum stands at local fêtes/shows

* lecture/talks programmes

* volunteer conservation group meetings

* recorded music programmes

* concerts

* organised fieldwork programmes

* photo-recording training/fieldwork

* multi-ethnic arts festivals

* oral history training/fieldwork

* talks and demonstrations by visiting specialists

* competitions and quizzes, prizegivings and associated exhibitions

* craft fairs/projects

*     publication launches

*     previews of exhibitions

*     hospital visiting programmes

*     dance and drama programmes

*     artist-in-residence schemes

*     pageants

These examples give an insight into the potential which leisure learning programmes provide for developing interest in the museum's work. Planning events and activities programmes can of course be time-consuming, and this has to be balanced against other areas of the museum's work. If the museum has a support group (see section 4.7), its involvement in such work can provide valuable opportunities for extending participation in the museum's work. Joint activities with other organisations is another way of sharing the load and at the same time can help to establish long-term working relationships for mutual advantage.

The success of leisure learning programmes depends on their being relevant to the museum's work and its collections, their quality and their effective marketing (see section 3.2). Desk research and discussion with other museums about the practicalities of setting up and managing leisure learning programmes will help you to develop your ideas. It may well be helpful to evaluate your leisure learning programmes, describing the steps taken and writing up the results in a manual. A leisure learning manual helps to avoid reinventing the wheel each time a similar activity is run, and allows the museum to build on previous experience in a systematic way.

*The success of leisure learning programmes depends on their being relevant to the museum's work and its collections, their quality and their effective marketing.*

## 3.9 ENQUIRIES AND RESEARCH FACILITIES

### Enquiries

Museums provide information for their users and respond to their enquiries in many different ways. All museums have to deal with enquiries, and users will ask many different sorts of question of the museum. The most common type of enquiry is the identification of objects, either at the museum or at another location. Other types of enquiry will include requests for information for school project work and for detailed information from research students and scholars. Your museum will also have to deal with a quite extraordinary range of general enquiries, some of which may at first sight appear to have little to do with the museum's work!

Museums have to develop policies to deal with these different types of enquiry, and staff need to know what procedures to follow. For example, an object brought into the museum for identification and left at the museum's reception desk will require special documentation procedures (see section 2.5), including a receipt for deposit and collection, a description of the object left at the desk, a written report on the object and a statement of the conditions under which the object has been accepted by the museum. These may include a condition that the museum does not provide valuations of objects, and accepts no responsibility for loss or damage or the accuracy of the written report. Procedures for looking after an item while it is in the museum's safekeeping or for sending an item to another museum or institution for specialist identification need to be established.

Answering questions or redirecting enquiries to another more appropriate institution in a helpful and sympathetic manner is an important service to your museum's users, whether over the telephone, in person or in writing. Answering enquiries can take time, and may on occasions appear to have only restricted benefit for the museum. In the long term, however, this aspect of work will build up the overall constituency of support for your museum. Many museum curators have been surprised, and not a little delighted, when an enquirer has donated an object which has been identified by the museum to the collections!

In the long term, this aspect of work will build up the overall constituency of support for your museum.

Logging enquiries systematically will help you to establish trends and identify what are the most common. One way to reduce time on common enquiries is to develop a range of standard leaflets and letters. With word-processors becoming more widely available, it is now possible to personalise or tailor a standard letter appropriately. It is important to remember however that a common enquiry in your museum may be the first time somebody has made contact with the museum. Do not give the impression that you are not interested in the enquiry. What may appear to be a straightforward enquiry can lead to significant long-term involvement with the museum!

### Research and scholarship

All museums have a responsibility to add to knowledge through research.

All museums have a responsibility to add to knowledge through research carried out by the museum's staff or by enabling others to use the museum's collections for research purposes. Making your collections available for research by students and scholars is an essential aspect of the museum's work. Specialist investigation or identification of objects in the collections is always to be encouraged, and museums should do all they can to develop research interest in their collections.

Do however be mindful of the security and conservation problems in allowing access to your collections by researchers. Check that researchers are bona fide and ensure that they are briefed on the appropriate care of the objects being studied, especially if they have to be handled. Every effort should be made to provide appropriate space for study purposes (see section 2.4). A clean and tidy area with tables and chairs, and good lighting is essential. It is *always* necessary to record items taken from storage or display for study purposes, and to check them off in detail against the record at the end of the study session with the researcher present, however well you know the researcher. Museum staff can then be sure that the items have not been mislaid or damaged during or after their study.

It is normal to expect appropriate acknowledgement in any publication based on collections research, and you may wish to draw up a standard form of acknowledgement for such study. Every effort should be made to obtain copies of articles or reports which include reference to the museum's collections. These will help place your own collections in a wider context and will form a valuable part of the documentation supporting the collection. Where information about the collections is published in this way, the museum should ensure that it is fed into its documentation system (see section 2.5).

### 3.10 SHOPS AND SALES POINTS

There are considerable opportunities for generating additional revenue income for your museum through establishing a shop or sales point. The design and layout of any retail outlet is an important first consideration. The function of a shop is to attract and sell - in volume. Too often museum shops or sales points present their goods in a dull and unimaginative way, with insufficient attention being paid to lighting, ease of access or quality of fittings. It is a pointless exercise to invest hard-earned capital in stock, and then to discourage its sale by poor presentation! In designing a shop or a sales point, do take professional advice, and have your outlet designed with sales, security and customer convenience firmly in mind. As with all areas of a new museum, it will be necessary to design your retail area taking access for disabled people into consideration.

## Location

The most effective location for your shop may be at the museum exit. Most sales on-site are made at the end of a visit, although visitors will need to have guiding literature available at the entrance to the museum. Location will depend to a large extent on staffing resources, and in a small museum you may find for practical reasons that your shop has to be sited at your entrance/exit point. If this is the case, care should be taken not to discourage sales by the movement of visitors entering and leaving through the sales area. Design and layout is therefore all important.

Design and layout is all important.

Do encourage the use of the shop in its own right if your building and visitor circulation allow it. Visiting the shop by itself can be an important source of additional income. There are however other ways of thinking about location. You may find that a second museum shop is possible in another location, for example, on the high street of your local town or within a larger shop, such as a department store. Alternatively, renting temporary high street premises for the Christmas period may give you additional income. It may be possible to consider a consortium approach and establish a trading company with a number of museums in the area. There are many possibilities, and imagination and experimentation can be useful in boosting income for the museum.

Another aspect of location is off-site sales and mail order, where the museum can extend its market well beyond its four walls. A good quality publications and sales list, with an order form, can be distributed very widely. Promotional opportunities exist through leisure learning programmes, magazines, joint mailings with other organisations, direct mailing, and the use of other outlets like tourist information centres. A publications and sales list need not be glossy or expensive to produce. With desk-top publishing systems, it is perfectly possible to produce an attractive list which can extend sales considerably.

**Stock**

The stock for your shop or sales point will be made up of items produced by the museum and/or items bought in from outside sources. Your stock range will depend on your available capital, but in starting up and managing new museums it is perhaps best to build up your stock gradually giving yourself time to find out what is or is not popular, what provides the best profit margin, and what is most effective in terms of your overall policy for retailing. Items produced by or for the museum and related to its work and collections will have the sales advantage of not being widely available outside the museum. Items bought in, such as souvenirs, publications and local craft items, should also be related to the museum's collections and its work. Whatever range of stock you invest in, ensure that the number of suppliers is kept as low as possible. This helps to reduce the management time and costs associated with the shop. All stock, whatever its size or type, should be of good design and good quality. It is also worthwhile investing in printed packaging which will help to publicise the museum and its shop.

Your pricing policy will depend amongst other things on production or wholesale costs, management costs, and discount and VAT requirements. It needs to be related in broad terms to market prices for similar items outside the museum. Collaboration between museums or other organisations in producing publications or postcards for example, or making joint purchases, can help to reduce costs.

In parallel with designing and developing your shop, the museum will need to lay down procedures for stock control and for monitoring daily and weekly cash takings (see section 4.3). Electronic till systems, which provide assistance in stock control procedures by storing information related to sales, are widely available and much time and trouble can be saved by investing in one of these at an early stage in development. Clean and secure storage for stock items is essential, and regular stock checks should be undertaken.

The museum shop is an important aspect of the museum's communications policy and has a key role to play in public relations.

The museum shop is an important aspect of the museum's communications policy and has a key role to play in public relations. It may be one of the few points of direct contact with museum staff during a visit. Efficient and courteous service on the part of staff makes for good public relations, and will help to increase takings. It also provides a further opportunity to learn more about your users (see section 3.2).

## 3.11 CATERING

Most museums with a little imagination and a relatively modest investment can provide some form of refreshment facility for their visitors. On a basic level, a filter coffee unit, disposable cups, and a sitting area with information about the museum and its programmes, can provide a welcome bonus to the tired and thirsty visitor. At a more sophisticated level, a self-service or table-service restaurant may be possible, depending on resources and visitor numbers. The spectrum is a wide one.

As a service to your visitors such provision, in a similar way to a shop or leisure learning programme, can encourage longer visits and attract additional income. The balance of expenditure and income needs to be carefully watched however, and it may well be preferable to build up your catering operation incrementally. As with your shop, it may be possible to plan a cafe or restaurant so that it attracts those not visiting the museum as well as your visitors. In this way the restaurant can be opened independently of the museum when needed, with obvious advantages.

Coffee-corner or cafe, restaurant or fast-food outlet, each deserves to be well designed, to have good quality food and drink, and to be fitted out with well-designed fixtures and fittings. The higher the standards of design, presentation and service, the more successful the facility will be. Many museums have the opportunity to 'theme' their refreshment areas by using design ideas derived from their collections. For example, a railway museum might recreate an early 1900s station restaurant for use as the museum cafe, a social history museum may use its restaurant as a way of demonstrating local or regional dishes, or a maritime museum may base its menus on locally caught seafood. The opportunities are endless, and for visitors can dramatically extend interest in their visit. A poor experience can equally destroy the pleasure of the visit and ensure that no return visit is made.

The higher the standards of design, presentation and service, the more successful the facility will be.

Catering for the public carries with it particular and often stringent legal requirements, and it will be necessary to ensure that hygiene standards are rigorously applied. The museum may employ its own catering staff or perhaps operate its catering facilities under franchise arrangements. It is helpful to visit other museums and visitor attractions and discuss the various pros and cons with their staff, and discuss your plans in advance with your local authority.

The provision of toilets and washbasins in new museums is a necessity for both staff and visitors. Numbers and type, 'male/female', will depend on your visitors, but need for example to take account of coach party visits, parents or carers with young children and disabled visitors. Their condition, as with the museum itself and its surrounds, should be kept immaculate at all times.

If for any reason you are unable to provide refreshment facilities, it is worthwhile providing information on their whereabouts in the vicinity of the museum. A simple map or leaflet providing these details can save considerable staff time in answering the same question time and time again. It may also be an opportunity to work with local businesses in mutual promotion schemes.

# 4 MANAGING THE MUSEUM

*'It is worth remembering that the success of your new museum will ultimately depend not on your visitors or your displays, but on the skills and abilities of those working for the museum. They are the most important resource of all.'*

## 4.1 MANAGING A NEW MUSEUM

In sections 1.10 and 1.11, we discussed the legal status of the new museum and the development of policy. In this section, the most appropriate ways of devising a management structure are described. There is a substantial body of experience in this area, and your Area Museum Council will be able to advise on appropriate structures in the light of Museum Registration requirements (see section 4.5) and charity legislation and procedures. The Area Museum Council will also be able to direct you to other museums which can provide guidance in the light of their own experience. The Museums Association through its various codes of conduct is another source of advice on best practice (see section 5.0).

### Trustees

The principal tasks of your Board of Trustees will be to determine the policy of the museum (see section 1.11) and to decide how the museum's income, both revenue and capital, should be spent in the context of the museum's forward plan. They will need to monitor and evaluate the progress which the museum is making against its planning objectives (see section 1.12), and ensure that financial support for the museum is forthcoming from a plurality of sources, for example admission charges, individual and corporate givers, local authorities, or your Area Museum Council. Honorary or paid staff will then carry out the policy determined by the Trustees and ensure that they are kept regularly informed of progress and external factors relevant to their decision-making.

The membership of your Board of Trustees will be influenced by the type of organisation or group of individuals who originally set up the museum. It should be borne in mind that a Board of Trustees appointed to manage the museum should not necessarily be made up of the same people who initiated the museum. The skills needed to manage the museum can be very different to those required to set up the museum in the first place. The two key requirements of Trustees are that they are wholly committed to the aims and objectives of the museum and its development, and are prepared and able to give freely of their time and energy to its work. The span of experience of your Trustees is also an important consideration. So, too, is their understanding of the legal and ethical responsibilities which they are undertaking, for a charitable

> The principal tasks of your Board of Trustees will be to determine the policy of the museum and to decide how the museum's income should be spent in the context of the museum's forward plan.

trust's funds and property are administered for the benefit of the public. This is an aspect of charity legislation which has come under increasing scrutiny in recent years and all Trustees need to be fully aware of their position in this respect.

A typical Board would include a Chairperson, an Honorary Secretary and an Honorary Treasurer and other invited persons. The Honorary Secretary might also be the executive director of the museum. These persons should be appointed on the basis of the quality of their judgement and depth of expertise, and on their commitment to the work of the Trust. The number of Trustees will vary from one Trust to another, although it is generally agreed that about twelve persons is an appropriate number.

In some cases, Trustees elect to establish a management committee from their number to provide closer supervision of the museum's day-to-day work. The disadvantages of this approach are that it becomes easy for Trustees to lose their sense of involvement in the direction and development of the museum. Trustees should be sufficiently committed to review the conduct and progress of the museum on a regular basis, say every two months, although it may be appropriate to delegate certain powers to the Chairman, Honorary Treasurer and Honorary Secretary if particular decisions need to be taken quickly outside the Trustees' normal cycle of meetings. It is also good practice to ensure that all Trustees retire on a rotation basis and that there is a set age limit for retirement which is adhered to.

The Trustees of a charity incorporated as a company are directors of that company for purposes of general company law and the Companies Act. If a museum is established as a company limited by guarantee, the management of the museum will differ to that of an unincorporated body governed by a Deed of Trust. A company limited by guarantee provides for members who are people subscribing to the company's Memorandum of Association. The size of the company can vary greatly, although it is as well to place a limit, perhaps 50, on the number of company members. Members, who may include nominees from other organisations such as local authorities, act in a similar way to the shareholders of a normal company in electing from their number the company's directors.

The company receives the Annual Report and annual accounts, which are a legal requirement and must be properly audited and filed at Companies' House within a set period. The Board of Directors is elected, following the requirements of the Memorandum of Association, and then has responsibility for the direction and management of the museum.

In drawing up a draft Deed of Trust or a memorandum and articles of association it is essential to take legal advice from a solicitor experienced in this area of work. Your Area Museum Council and the Museums and Galleries Commission will also advise on the draft for the purposes of meeting Museum Registration requirements.

Because of the complexity of trusteeship, it is useful to establish a manual for each trustee which might include for example guidance on legal responsibilities, financial responsibilities, agreed policies and procedures, details of forward planning objectives, nationally agreed codes of conduct for Trustees of museums, in particular the Museums Association's Code of Practice for Museum Authorities and Guidelines for Committee Members, and copies of minutes of Board papers and reports. A manual ensures that each Trustee has at his or her fingertips information and reference material relevant to the decision-making process.

### Committees

It is a widespread practice to establish a number of working groups or sub-committees to help develop particular aspects of the museum's work and advise on policy matters. These should be chaired by members of the Board, but might include other individuals from professional bodies who are able to bring their expertise to bear on the museum's work. Such groups might include for example:

* a Development Group responsible for raising capital funds for the museum. The tasks of such a group would be to help secure necessary funds from individual or corporate donors and grant-giving bodies, to carry through specific development programmes (see section 4.4).

* a User Services or a Communications Group responsible for advising the Trustees on policy for developing user services and facilities (see section 3.3).

* an Administration Group responsible for advising the Trustees on policy about the museum's administrative and financial work (see sections 4.3 and 4.10).

* a Curatorial Group responsible for advising the Trustees on collections and collecting and disposal policies, conservation and documentation, scholarship and research (see section 2.1).

The establishment of such groups to a large extent depends on the numbers of professional staff in the museum. The groups above, which reflect four key areas of the museum's work, would draw on the expertise of Trustees as well as individuals from outside organisations supporting the work of the museum. Professional or honorary staff would work closely with these groups in helping to develop policy proposals, and then carry out programmes of action agreed by the Trustees in the context of the museum's forward plan. It is vital, however, in establishing such committee structures that lines of accountability and areas of responsibility are clearly defined. There is always a danger that particular committees will take decisions beyond their remit, and this can create difficulties between the Board and the committee. In establishing committees to support its work, the Board must be quite clear about respective responsibilities to secure maximum advantage from its support structure.

> It is vital in establishing committee structures that lines of accountability and areas of responsibility are clearly defined.

## 4.2 MANAGING BUILDINGS

Museum buildings come in all shapes and sizes. In some cases, they have been custom-built for museum purposes, in other cases, buildings which were never constructed with the museum function in mind have been adapted to their new use - with varying degrees of success.

In developing new museum buildings for public access there are a number of procedural steps which should be followed. Some of these we have already touched on in earlier sections of this book and these should be referred to for further detail. The outline steps are:

1. Examine the basic objectives and constraints of the museum building project

2 Relate the museum building programme to the museum's forward plan

3. Identify space and facilities required for collections management

4. Establish the market context for the new museum building

5. Identify space and facilities required for the museum's users

6. Undertake feasibility assessment in the light of above

7. Establish funding requirements and fund-raising programme

8. Brief architect and designer

Most new museums are housed in existing buildings modified for museum use. While the above steps are in the first instance appropriate for new museum buildings, they are also relevant for examining buildings for conversion purposes. In considering converting existing buildings for museum use, it is imperative to analyze the full range of functions for which the building will be used (steps 3 and 5 above), to examine these functions against the space available in the building proposed for reuse, and to decide in the light of your analysis whether the building conversion costs can be justified in terms of the proposed use (step 6).

It may well be that although a building deserves to be saved or restored, its use as a museum is neither practicable or cost-effective, and an alternative approach is needed. This may require assessment of other buildings or the construction of a new building which can often be more cost-effective in the long-term if maintenance costs have to be taken into account. It is surprisingly common to find that in order to save a historic building from destruction, its use as a museum has been recommended without adequate consideration of the functions which a museum carries out, without consideration of the market context in which a museum will operate and without consideration of the operational costs which its managing body will need to find. A significant amount of public and private money can be wasted on inappropriate conversions for museum use.

The quality of service which any museum can provide will depend to a large extent on the space available to carry out its work effectively. This does not mean that all new museums should be large, but that their function should be the principal consideration in deciding on how

The quality of service which any museum can provide will depend to a large extent on the space available to carry out its work effectively.

they should be housed. Assessing buildings, new or old, in a systematic way against the functions intended for them does two main things - gives the client a clear indication of the aims of the museum building project, the resources required and the structure of the necessary work programme; and provides a basis of communication between clients, and architects, designers, conservation specialists, contractors and funding bodies.

**Briefing**

In building a new museum, or converting existing buildings for museum use, you will need professional guidance from an architect. It is important to recognise that the architect will also need professional guidance from you in the form of first, an outline brief and later, a detailed brief. The value of undertaking the steps outlined above is that they will help to develop the background information necessary for effective briefing. In drawing up a brief for an architect, who will later be responsible for briefing contractors to undertake the range of work to be carried out, a great deal of clear thinking and hard work is required. It is essential to be realistic about the amount of time needed in drawing up briefs for architects and designers (see section 3.5). The brief will essentially be the basis of your contract with your architect and needs to give him or her a clear idea of the purpose and functions of the building, the spatial requirements for different aspects of the museum's work, and the constraints under which the project will be operating, especially finance, time, and planning and legal considerations.

In drawing up a brief for an architect, a great deal of clear thinking and hard work is required.

In selecting an architect for your project, you should examine what similar projects the architectural practice and the architect have carried out in previous years and what body of experience exists within the practice. Sound out past clients about the quality of service provided, for example, imaginative use of space, cost controls, snagging problems, building efficiency and time management. Guidance in choosing and briefing architects can be obtained from your Area Museum Council and the various architects' professional associations in the UK.

The various relationships between director/curator, Trustees, designer, conservation adviser, and architect need to be worked out and agreed, and the respective roles of the team of people involved in bringing the project to a satisfactory conclusion need to be clearly defined.

## Maintenance

All museum buildings need a maintenance regime, internally and externally. It is good practice to establish as part of your administrative procedures a regular check of the building and its fixtures and fittings to monitor wear and tear. Decisions can then be taken in good time to replace fixtures or fittings, or carry out routine maintenance such as painting. The same approach needs to be taken to the outside of the building, and its environs. This can be more expensive to carry out thoroughly. For example, regular inspection of roof areas, guttering, paintwork may necessitate scaffolding or specialist contractors. However, in the long run, maintenance procedures such as these can save considerable amounts of money by identifying problems at an early date. Preventive conservation starts from outside your museum building!

Maintenance procedures can save considerable amounts of money by identifying problems at an early date.

## 4.3 MANAGING FINANCES/RUNNING COSTS

Establishing and managing a new museum is in many ways similar to setting up and running a business. Your original feasibility assessment will have examined the financial requirements in some detail, both in terms of capital and revenue income and expenditure or operating costs. That preparatory work will have identified in detail the financial responsibilities which the museum will have to meet, and provided preliminary cash-flow forecasts in terms of operating costs and income. Here we are concerned with how best to manage the finances of the museum.

The museum's forward plan should incorporate a financial plan which is the financial mechanism by which the museum's forward planning objectives are driven forward.

The museum's forward plan should incorporate a financial plan which is the financial mechanism by which the museum's forward planning objectives are driven forward. The financial plan should provide a structured budget showing heads of expenditure, anticipated income, and cash-flow forecasts. It is an essential component of your overall forward plan. Drawing up a financial plan provides both a framework for action in helping you to estimate what you will be able to afford to undertake, and also allows potential funding bodies to assess your intentions and the financial viability of the new museum.

## An example of the structure of a revenue budget

| Revenue expenditure | Estimate | Actual | Revenue income | Estimate | Actual |
|---|---|---|---|---|---|
| *Museum management* | | | admissions to | | |
| staff salaries/wages + | | | museum | | |
| National Insurance | | | membership | | |
| superannuation | | | subscriptions | | |
| travelling expenses | | | grants | | |
| building maintenance | | | donations | | |
| rates | | | museum shop | | |
| electricity/water/gas | | | museum catering | | |
| insurance | | | events programme | | |
| cleaning/cleaning | | | services e.g. lectures | | |
| materials | | | sponsorship | | |
| security | | | loans | | |
| telephone | | | | | |
| postage and stationery | | | **totals** | **total** | **total** |
| office equipment | | | | *estimated* | *actual* |
| depreciation | | | | *income* | *income* |
| interest charges/ | | | | | |
| repayments on | | | | | |
| loans | | | | | |
| miscellaneous/ | | | | | |
| contingency | | | | | |
| | | | | | |
| *collections management* | | | | | |
| conservation/ | | | | | |
| conservation | | | | | |
| materials | | | | | |
| storage/storage | | | | | |
| materials | | | | | |
| documentation/ | | | | | |
| documentation | | | | | |
| materials | | | | | |
| equipment | | | | | |
| insurance | | | | | |
| purchase fund | | | | | |
| | | | | | |
| *public services* | | | | | |
| shop stock | | | | | |
| catering | | | | | |
| marketing/publicity | | | | | |
| publications | | | | | |
| education materials | | | | | |
| **totals** | **total** | **total** | **BALANCE** | *Profit +* | *Profit +* |
| | *estimated* | *actual* | | *loss –* | *loss –* |
| | *expenditure* | *expenditure* | | | |

The first step in financial planning is to draw up a budget with the estimated costs which will arise from the museum's work and the estimated income. In business terms this is termed a 'profit and loss' budget or revenue budget, and examines the relationship between money earned (revenue income) and money spent (revenue expenditure). In order to run the museum efficiently, it is clear that the revenue expenditure should not exceed the revenue income within any one financial year. On the basis of your earlier investigations and discussions with advisers, it should be possible to draw up a fairly accurate picture of the anticipated outgoings or expenditure of the museum and establish cash-flow projections.

It is advisable to discuss your budget and financial planning with a qualified accountant who will be able to provide guidance on financial recording and taxation. It may also be possible to obtain assistance in this aspect of your work from economic development agencies or local authorities providing small business advisory services. If the museum is managed as a limited company, annual returns and audited accounts will need to be submitted to the Registrar of Companies and other such requirements must be complied with under the Companies Act. Formal responsibility for managing the finances of the museum is best placed in the hands of one person, normally an Honorary Treasurer, who has appropriate experience in financial matters. The Honorary Treasurer would be expected to report to the museum's Board on financial management on a regular basis, and present financial monitoring statements. The Board as a whole is responsible for the museum's accounts being properly audited at the end of the financial year.

Monitoring procedures should be established so that monthly statements of actual expenditure/income can be drawn up and compared against the museum's estimated income/expenditure and its cash-flow forecasts. In order for these to be drawn up accurately, as well as for security reasons, monitoring procedures for daily and weekly cash takings need to be set up. Financial procedures such as these should be written down in a financial manual which can form part of a broader administrative manual (see section 4.10). In this way, the museum can provide for consistency and continuity in this important aspect of its work.

## Budgets

The headings in the outline annual revenue budget given here are provided for guidance. They can be broken down in further detail, and there are various ways of assigning headings given under 'museum management' to discrete cost centres. For example, it would be possible to assign all costs associated with education to an education cost centre, including a percentage of fixed costs such as rates or building maintenance, staff costs, supplies and services, travel and subsistence and so on. Whatever structure of budget your museum opts for, these headings provide categories of expenditure that all new museums will have to cater for (see page 105).

Drawing up a realistic, monthly cash-flow projection will help to break down the overall annual estimates in finer detail, and show how income and expenditure can be expected to fluctuate during the year. This helps to set up early warning systems in the case of unforeseen problems, and allows the museum's monthly monitoring statements to be compared against monthly estimates. There is a considerable range of computer software for financial management now on the market, and it may help to invest in a software package for your computer for these purposes.

A clear idea of what pattern your revenue income and expenditure will take through the year is a vital part of financial planning. For example, the seasonal nature of the tourist trade in many parts of the UK may well mean that revenue income from tourist visitors rises sharply in the spring and summer months and falls away in the autumn and winter. Such changes in the level of income can be estimated on the basis of others' experience and incorporated into your cash-flow forecasting. Another example is the need to remember that some bills are paid at different times of the year. You will have to meet some bills in quarterly instalments, for example telephone bills, and some in advance, for example insurance. You may also have to pay the full cost of projects or equipment which have been grant-aided by national or regional agencies, before claiming the grant. These variations in cash-flow therefore need to be predicted to ensure that the museum does not incur financial penalties from the bank. It will be helpful to annotate your cash-flow projections with information as to how you have drawn up the projections, and what assumptions underlie them, for future reference and comparison.

A clear idea of what pattern your revenue income and expenditure will take through the year is a vital part of financial planning.

## 4.4 FUND RAISING/CAPITAL PROJECTS

For new museums, feasibility assessment will have explored the capital costs associated with different aspects of the museum, for example building work and architect's fees, displays and designer's fees, equipment, furnishings and fittings. These one-off costs or capital costs have different fund-raising requirements to operating costs, and these are discussed below. The capital costs associated with starting up a new museum should be very carefully analyzed as part of feasibility assessment. Phasing the development programme over a number of years may help to spread costs.

The capital costs associated with starting up a new museum should be very carefully analyzed as part of feasibility assessment.

### Raising capital funds

Raising finance to cover the capital costs of a new museum deserves detailed study and there are a number of sources of information which provide guidance on procedures and practice (see section 6.0). Support agencies such as your Area Museum Council, the Museums and Galleries Commission, economic development agencies and tourist boards, which help fund new museum developments, will provide written guidelines about the nature and extent of their funding support. It is well worth discussing at an early stage of your thinking what help the museum might be eligible for through grants or loans. You should be aware that while a scheme or project may be eligible for funding, this does not guarantee financial support. Most grant-giving agencies, whether in the public sector or in the charitable sector, have far more applications for their support than they can provide funding help for.

It is important to ensure that application for funding support is made within the deadlines set for applications, and that all the necessary detail is provided. Your fund-raising strategy needs to take account of deadlines for grant applications and the likely response time from the funding body. Normally grants from national or regional agencies will be provided on a matching or top-up basis, and will always have a range of conditions attached to them, which must be adhered to. It is important to make sure in advance of application that the conditions of grant can be met, otherwise a great deal of time can be wasted on all sides. Another point to remember is that often grants are given on completion of work which has been paid for and for which invoices are available. Your cash-flow needs to take this into consideration.

## The case for support

Whatever your project, whether it is for building work or equipment, fees for specialists or renewal programmes, a carefully costed presentation of the project for which you are seeking support is essential. The better your project is presented on paper and in person, the better chance you have of a favourable response. Fund-raising from national agencies or charitable trusts, local authorities or individuals, needs to be carefully thought through and your case for support carefully prepared. Given the scale of competition for funding for new museum projects, a well prepared and vigorous fund-raising campaign will be essential. It is generally agreed that a Development Committee (see section 4.1), charged with responsibility for fund-raising and chaired by an influential individual with direct access to senior levels of business or industrial organisations is a valuable asset for your Board.

In raising substantial sums, say £100,000 plus, 80% is likely to come from a relatively small number of supporters in the 'giving pyramid'. This is however not to ignore the importance of the 'small givers'. They may be prepared to support the museum through taking part in an imaginative events programme and to play a vital role in raising financial support by encouraging others to participate. Community support for a new museum project can often be a powerful means of unlocking local authority support, and through this, support from other agencies.

Fund-raising to be effective is very time-consuming, and can carry significant expenses. If fund-raising is carried out on a voluntary basis, rather than through professional staff or fund-raising consultants, it needs to be very carefully programmed to maximize the efforts being made on behalf of the new museum. Volunteers involved in raising funds, perhaps through the museum's Friends' organisation, need to be well coordinated, thoroughly briefed and if necessary trained in their task. At the same time, they need to be rewarded by knowing that their efforts are valued and that the funds which they raise are being put to effective use within the museum's forward planning.

It is equally essential that all donors, whether in kind or in cash, are kept regularly informed of progress in the new museum development. Good public relations are a vitally important factor in fund-raising. Your

The better your project is presented on paper and in person, the better chance you have of a favourable response.

Good public relations are a vitally important factor in fund-raising.

donors, whether they are commercial companies, grant-giving trusts, local authorities or private individuals, are a key constituency of support and you may well wish to go back to them on a number of occasions in succeeding years for further help.

A number of new museums have created separate Development Trusts specifically to raise funds for their development programme. Although there can be strengths in this approach, there are also weaknesses. The trustees of the Development Trust raising capital for project developments may for example not always agree with the museum's trustees on how this money should be spent. Development Trusts can also be expensive to set up and administer, and care needs to be exercised in setting up such a separate entity. There is no legal or charitable reason for a separate Development Trust to be established.

There are advantages and disadvantages too in employing fund-raising consultants, whose fees are normally met by a percentage of the funds raised for your project. In deciding whether to employ a particular firm of fund-raising consultants, it is as well to discuss with previous clients in a similar situation what quality of service they have received and what results were achieved. If you decide to use fund-raising consultants, they will need to be fully briefed on the aims and objectives of the museum, its development programme, and to what purposes money raised will be put.

In the case of raising money through commercial sponsorship, it is of paramount importance to define in detail what business benefits a commercial sponsor might obtain from the museum for his or her support. Sponsorship should not be confused with patronage - it is a business relationship with value and benefit to both sides. Never undersell what the museum has to offer by way of benefits to your sponsor.

There is an extensive literature on fund-raising and sponsorship for museums (see section 5.0). Much of this material provides case-study examples of good practice in fund-raising and a little research can make a great deal of difference to the quality of your fund-raising programmes.

## 4.5 MUSEUM REGISTRATION AND STANDARDS

### Museum Registration

The Museums and Galleries Commission introduced a national Museum Registration scheme to all parts of the United Kingdom in 1988 with the assistance of the ten Area Museum Councils. The scheme, which is voluntary, has been adjudged a significant success and has helped to raise standards in a number of key areas of responsibility, such as collections documentation and access to professional curatorial advice. It has helped progressively museums of all types and sizes to improve standards of operation and to demonstrate to funding bodies of all types that they are worthy of investment and support.

Museum Registration is a minimum standards scheme. Its main requirements are:

* conformity with the Museums Association definition of a museum (see section 1.1b), or if appropriate, the Museums and Galleries Commission's definition of a 'national' museum;

* an acceptable constitution;

* an acceptable statement of collections management policy;

* a range of public services and facilities for visitors which are appropriate to the type and size of museum;

* access to professional curatorial advice;

* an acceptable financial basis, and compliance with legal, planning and safety requirements.

Museum Registration is now recognised as a national minimum standard for museums in the United Kingdom. It helps museums of all types and sizes demonstrate that they share a common basis of operation. A museum must be on the national Museum Register to be eligible for grant-aid or subsidised services from the Museums and Galleries Commission or the Area Museum Councils. This helps to show that museums in receipt of public funding is being used in an effective and responsible way. Museum Registration is recommended as one of a number of criteria for auditing local authority museums and

Museum Registration is now recognised as a national minimum standard for museums in the United Kingdom.

for local authority support for independent museums. The Museum Register is also increasingly being used by public agencies and charitable organisations as a guide for their funding support.

It is important that all Registered Museums promote the fact that they are non-profit bodies, have a long-term purpose, and manage and use their collections in a responsible way. Every effort is being made by the Museums and Galleries Commission and the Area Museum Councils to promote the scheme to public audiences so that the value and benefits of Museum Registration can be widely recognised.

The Museums and Galleries Commission identifies the advantages of Museum Registration in the following ways:

* the fostering of confidence among potential donors that a registered museum is a suitable repository;

* the opportunity for a museum to promote itself as an organisation providing a basic range of services for the benefit of its users;

* eligibility for grant-aid from the Museums and Galleries Commission and the Area Museum Councils;

* and the fostering of confidence among other funding agencies and organisations that a registered museum is worthy of support.

Museum Registration is a benchmark for museums in the United Kingdom.

Museum Registration is therefore a benchmark for museums in the United Kingdom. Its welcome by the museums industry and the large number of museums now registered demonstrate its success. Guidelines and application forms are available from your Area Museum Council or the Museums and Galleries Commission.

### Standards

In recent years, standards in museum work have become of increasing importance. The minimum standards of the Museum Registration scheme are one example. Others include optimum standards in the care of archaeological, geological and biological collections, and new customer care standards which have been developed by the Museums and Galleries Commission (see section 5.0). Of particular importance are the new standards developed by the Museum Training Institute as the Industry Lead Body which form the agreed industry standards for many aspects of museum work.

Standards fall broadly into two groups - corporate and personal. Museum Registration is an example of the former, while the Museum Training Institute's standards have been drawn up in conjunction with people working throughout the museums industry to demonstrate the standards of work which should be achievable at different levels. Measuring your museum or yourself against agreed, industry-wide standards, allows comparison to be made between institutions and individuals. Where investment decisions are having to be made this objective approach is of value to funding bodies, museums themselves and the individuals working in and for them.

Standards are closely linked to performance measurement. Museums can establish their own standards or use standards which have been developed externally. Measuring performance against standards can assist managers and individual staff members in gauging the success of their institution and their own achievements.

*Measuring performance against standards can assist managers and individual staff members in gauging the success of their institution and their own achievements.*

The Museum Training Institute's standards are being used as the basis of new qualifications systems within the industry. In future, it is likely that training provision will be increasingly standards-related, with the individual's ability or competence to carry out tasks judged against standards set in different aspects of museum work. This type of skills assessment will have a major impact on museum development over the next decade, and those managing museums should keep up-to-date with developments in this area.

## 4.6 MANAGING PEOPLE - STAFF

A key question facing all new museum developments, particularly small charitable trust museums, is whether or not to employ professional staff, that is to say people with experience of working in museums with professional qualifications in museum management and museum work. Whatever the size of your museum, the basic tasks are the same and need to be carried out to professional standards (see section 4.5). Professional guidance in the work of the museum will not only increase confidence in its development and help to ensure that the museum's range of responsibilities are met, but also help to develop the museum effectively along professional lines.

*Whatever the size of your museum, the basic tasks are the same and need to be carried out to professional standards.*

Many of those working in a voluntary capacity in independent museums find themselves unable to carry out the necessary work

Managing museums
effectively can take a very
significant amount of time
and experience.

adequately due to their other interests or work. Managing museums effectively can take a very significant amount of time and experience. Professional staffing can ensure that the museum meets its responsibilities, and can provide professional supervision for volunteer helpers so that professional standards are met. Having a professional curator to coordinate the museum's forward planning and take responsibility for the day-to-day management of the museum can free supporters to utilise their skills in the most appropriate ways.

Access to professional advice for independent museums can be obtained under the national Museum Registration scheme through the museum's curatorial adviser, where no professional staff are employed (see section 4.5) and through your Area Museum Council, which will be itself able to provide a wide range of professional advice and assist in identifying other sources of specialist help as required. Your Area Museum Council will also be able to assist in the appointment of professional staff through advice over recruitment, job descriptions, conditions of service, contracts and interviewing, and may also provide pump-priming grants towards salary costs. Much thought needs to be given as to whether your museum can be effectively managed without professional staffing.

Apart from a professional curator, your Board may wish to appoint other in-house staff to carry out technical or clerical work. Much may depend on the availability of voluntary support for these activities. The larger the museum, however, the greater the demand for clerical and secretarial work in particular and volunteers may find it hard to provide an appropriate level of continuity and consistency in these areas of work. It is important that curatorial staff do not become encumbered with routine secretarial or clerical work, and devote their energies to the key tasks for which they have been appointed.

All permanent staff appointed should be provided with a contract of employment. Permanent and voluntary staff should have written job descriptions, so that each member of staff is fully aware of what they are required to do. This approach instils a sense of purpose in staff and helps to define how necessary tasks will be carried out.

### Temporary staff

It may be possible for the museum to engage temporary staff through employment training schemes or student placements. It is worth exploring what help can be obtained through employment training programmes from Training and Enterprise Councils or in Scotland, Local Enterprise Companies. A number of Universities providing training in museum studies, such as Leicester University, work with museums on placement schemes for their students and this can be a valuable source of temporary support.

However, if temporary staff are to carry out work effectively in the museum, they must have professional guidance and it is important that they receive on-going professional supervision. It will be important that work programmes devised by the museum provide training opportunities for the individuals concerned, and these will need to be discussed fully with the sponsoring agencies. Skills training in a variety of areas is a valuable and practical benefit which museums can offer trainees, although these skills will depend on the type of museum involved. Devising a work programme for temporary staff should always take into consideration the amount of time they have available. Half-finished projects are helpful to neither trainees nor the museum.

*If temporary staff are to carry out work effectively in the museum, they must have professional guidance.*

## 4.7 MANAGING PEOPLE - VOLUNTEERS AND FRIENDS' GROUPS

### Volunteers

Volunteers represent a valuable source of additional help to museums. They can support many different aspects of museum work. In small museums, the entire operation may be run by volunteers from Trustee to reception staff, fundraisers to curatorial staff. In larger museums, volunteers will find themselves working alongside paid, professional staff. Volunteers should in these circumstances not be used as a substitute for the work of paid staff. It is important that close consultation and agreement should take place with professional staff about the ways in which volunteers can be most effectively used to support and complement their work in the museum.

*Volunteers represent a valuable source of additional help to museums.*

Many independent museums make use of volunteers. Where the museum does have paid professional staff, it is generally considered inappropriate for volunteers to be carrying out core curatorial or management duties, such as documentation or security. It is better to direct volunteers to involve themselves in work which complements core responsibilities such as local history recording, photographic surveys, customer care and so on. Much will depend on the scale of the museum.

The museum should establish clear lines of responsibility when managing volunteers. The museum's managers should draw up firm policy guidelines over volunteer work and job descriptions so that it is quite clear what is expected of a volunteer. Not only is this important for volunteers who can then understand what is expected of them, but it is also important for the museum - with or without professional staff -which then has a consistent framework within which to manage volunteers. Where volunteers are being employed by the museum, it is equally important that they receive appropriate induction to the museum and its work, and training as appropriate. Training should be carried out as far as possible 'on the job', and your Area Museum Council will be able to assist with basic training support for volunteer groups. It is essential that volunteers are not required to carry out certain tasks, for example remedial conservation, unless under strict, professional supervision. Remedial conservation should only normally be carried out by trained and qualified conservators, but it may be possible for volunteers to provide support to professional conservators in different aspects of museum work. For registered museums without professional curatorial staff, your curatorial adviser will be able to advise on these issues.

Most volunteers will be prepared to devote considerable time and energy to help the museum in its work. Choosing and selecting volunteers for the tasks in hand can be a complex task, especially if there is interest in one or two areas of museum work but not in others where the need lies. If volunteers are to have a rewarding experience from their involvement with your museum and at the same time contribute usefully to its work, the museum's managers must recognise the need for effective selection and training. Managing volunteers can be a time-consuming task, especially if they have not been well selected in the first place. If volunteers do not carry out their tasks to an appropriate standard, or do not appear at the agreed time for work, then procedures need to be in place to remove them.

You should ensure that the organisation and management of volunteers is carried out to the same standard as paid staff. Effective coordination in these areas is vital, and one person, properly accountable to the museum's management, should have direct responsibility for coordinating the voluntary effort. Detailed guidance on the organisation of volunteer groups in museums is given in the various publications cited in sections 5 and 6.

### Friends' and support groups

There are a number of different ways in which people can participate in the work of the museum. We have noted the important contribution which volunteers can make to the day-to-day work of the museum above. A Friends' Group is another. While some Friends may also be volunteers, it is likely that most will be content to support the museum financially and in return receive a range of benefits - invitations to social events, to private views of exhibitions, concessions, publications and special events and activities. Friends' Groups represent an important constituency of support for museums throughout the United Kingdom. Museums of all sizes and types have established Friends' Groups with lasting benefit.

As with volunteers however, Friends' Groups need to be structured and managed effectively, as a poorly managed and organised group can have an adverse effect on the museum it should be supporting. Much advice on the establishment and management of Friends' Groups is available from the British Association of Friends of Museums (see section 6.0). It is advisable to make contact with existing Friends' Groups supporting museums of a type similar to your own before establishing a Group for your museum, and learning from their experience.

**Friends' Groups need to be structured and managed effectively,**

Some important areas for consideration are:

* constitution

* relationship with museum, and its Development Committee

* membership and recruitment

* information services - newsletter, bulletins

* events programmes

* promotion and marketing

* operational costs

* accounting and audit procedures

* identifiable benefits to the museum

Ensure that the servicing of a Friends' Group is not a drain on the museum's finances, and that it is wholly self-supporting. The primary task of a Friends' Group is to support the museum, not the reverse!

The work carried out by different Friends' Groups varies considerably. Hosting social occasions in the museum for potential donors, or to thank donors; raising money for specific purchases for the museum collections or for prizes for competitions; helping to subsidise the museum's newsletter; organising and financing exhibition previews; helping to run events and activities programmes are just some of the ways in which Friends' Groups can help museums. An additional benefit comes through being able to demonstrate that you are engaging with your local community in a variety of ways, and this can have a powerful effect on the ways in which patrons perceive your museum.

## 4.8 TRAINING AND PERSONAL DEVELOPMENT

All museums have a responsibility to establish a training and personal development policy and to train and develop their staff whether professional or voluntary. Although all those involved with the museum will bring with them a particular range of experience, as well as skills and qualifications, it is up to the museum's management to identify where training support is required and to provide it. The availability of 'in-service' training will encourage all staff to assess their own competence against industry standards appropriate to their area of work which have been developed by the Museum Training Institute, and identify with their managers their strengths and weaknesses (see section 4.5). The choice of training programmes to meet their needs can then be made. The benefits of an on-going training programme will be felt both in the museum and by the museum's users.

There are many training opportunities available for those working in museums at different levels. The spectrum is a wide one and much will depend on the type of training required. For example, general training courses in such areas as word-processing or customer care skills can be obtained from a variety of training organisations in the public and private sector. Such training is widely available. There are many training opportunities in technical, commercial, administrative or managerial work which can complement professional museum training courses.

In terms of professional training, your Area Museum Council will not only provide training courses in different aspects of museum work, but its training officer will be able to suggest other sources of training provision. The courses, conferences and meetings organised by Area Museum Councils and professional museum organisations, such as Museum Federations and Specialist Groups, can be used as building blocks within your training programmes. One of the key benefits for museum staff taking part in these training and development activities is the opportunity to meet others working in museums and share their experience.

There is also a variety of post-graduate and in-service courses available from museum studies departments in universities. Some of these can be taken on an in-service or part-time basis and provide professional qualifications for museum staff. Details of university courses providing professional training programmes in different aspects of museum work are given in the Museums Association Yearbook, and the Museums Journal carries regular information about short courses (see section 6).

If you are constructing training programmes on a modular basis from what is available and accessible to you to meet specific needs, it is worth remembering that visits to other museums and similar facilities to talk to staff and see new developments at first hand should be an important component. Reading programmes are also important, and your Area Museum Council will help to direct you to books, journals and other source material. There is a very wide range of material about museums and their work published every year. Keeping up-to-date with what is happening in the museum world is of critical importance, and will help you to assess your own museum's performance.

The success of your museum will ultimately depend not on your users, or your displays, but on the skills and abilities of those working for the museum. They are the most important resource you have, and training will help them to develop their skills and abilities for the benefit of all.

The success of your museum will ultimately depend not on your users, or your displays, but on the skills and abilities of those working for the museum.

## 4.9 HEALTH AND SAFETY

There have been significant changes in health and safety legislation in recent years bringing the UK in line with European Community requirements. Employers are legally responsible for providing a safe and healthy place of work for their employees under the Health and Safety at Work Act, 1974 (see section 4.2). Managers of new museums should have a written statement of policy regarding health and safety matters, and this should be issued to all members of staff. A copy should be posted in a prominent place in the museum for all to refer to. The museums's policy statement should include information on individuals' areas or responsibility, induction procedures for new staff, welfare, for example, cleaning, lighting, heating, and clothing, first-aid and accident report procedures, visitors and contractors working in the museum, and fire and disaster procedures.

Different types of museum will have special requirements. For example, museums with working machinery should make early contact with the Factories Inspectorate to discuss particular requirements in health and safety matters. Mining museums will need to make contact with the Mines Inspectorate; railway museums will need to take advice from the Railways Inspectorate. The nature of your museum will determine your health and safety policy.

Each member of staff should be actively involved in safety, health and welfare considerations.

One person, the museum's Health and Safety Officer, should have overall responsibility for monitoring how the museum's policy is implemented, and one individual should be responsible for the day-to-day aspects of health and safety in the museum. Each member of staff should be actively involved in safety, health and welfare considerations and be encouraged to draw any hazard or potential hazard to the attention of the museum's Health and Safety Officer. It may be necessary to assign responsibility for particular areas of the museum such as storage areas, workshops, or display galleries to different members of staff.

All new members of staff, including volunteers working in the museum, should be shown the layout of the museum's buildings and fire exits, as well as the location of fire-fighting equipment. Information on fire prevention and instructions on what to do in the case of fire are of paramount importance. Fire instructions and signs should be displayed clearly in all areas of the museum for staff and visitors alike. Training in first-aid to help deal with accidents in the museum is another aspect of the museum's health and safety policy which should be considered in depth. It is advisable to have trained first-aiders on the staff at all times.

Many accidents can be prevented by developing awareness of health and safety in staff through training and regular drills. The museum's Health and Safety Officer should be constantly concerned to increase such awareness, and should keep up to date with new UK and European legislation likely to affect the museum.

Contact with the local ambulance and fire service in the context of disaster planning procedures will also allow their personnel to maintain details of the museum's location and access in case of call-out. Such forward planning can save precious seconds in the case of an emergency or accident.

## 4.10 ADMINISTRATIVE PROCEDURES

A new museum will need to develop a number of administrative procedures to ensure efficient day-to-day running. In order to ensure consistency, and in the case of staff changes, continuity, it is well worth developing an administrative manual detailing the museum's various administrative procedures. Such a manual would include written and agreed procedures for all key aspects of the museum's administrative work, such as cash-handling and banking arrangements, invoicing and accounting, notification of staff sickness, staff briefing and induction, filling staff vacancies, stock control, agendas and minutes for committee meetings, and so on. Writing down the procedure for all of this work step-by-step helps to ensure that each time a particular administrative task is carried out, it is carried out in the same way. Where there are staff changes, or tasks are reassigned from one individual to another, the procedure can be learnt quickly and efficiently. It is not carried away inside someone's head, and the wheel does not have to be reinvented!

Although at first sight this may seem overly bureaucratic, it is a tried and tested approach to routine administration for museums of all sizes. Provided that the procedures are kept as straightforward as possible, a manual will save time and avoid confusion. From the point of view of

It is well worth developing an administrative manual detailing the museum's various administrative procedures.

the museum's management, a procedure manual has the added advantage of providing a ready-made training guide for new administrative staff.

## 4.11 COMPUTERS

Computers are now used for a very wide variety of tasks in museums, and new museums should examine their computer requirements at an early date. There are many tried and tested applications for computers in museums, in the fields of collections management and care, management and administration and user services. For example, computers are used extensively in collections management (see section 2.5), allowing for rapid data retrieval and the listing and indexing of collections records, and for logging environmental data in display and storage areas. In museum management and administration computers are used for financial management purposes, stock control and word-processing. In the museum's display areas, computers as components in desk-top publishing systems can help to reduce design costs and are increasingly being used for interactive purposes providing opportunities for visitors to explore collections in greater depth.

Information technology is under constant development and the computer marketplace is accordingly complex. It follows that a museum should carefully assess its computer requirements and the software it requires before making what can be significant investment. Compatibility with other systems, for example in the field of collections documentation, is likely to be of critical importance. A needs analysis carried out by computer consultants is a useful and practical first step. The implementation of their recommendations can then be phased into the museum's forward planning.

Computers are essentially tools helping to speed up tasks and allowing rapid access to data, whether this is text-based, or in audio or video format. Graphic designers have been able to use the enormous power of the new information technology to present information in dynamic new ways, and the presentation of computerised information in text or image format is likely to transform museum exhibitions and displays in the next ten-twenty years. As the technology develops, visitors to museums will be able to carry computerised information with them in

New museums should examine their computer requirements at an early date.

the gallery to provide additional interpretation for the collections on view. Such developments will have a powerful impact on communication practice in museums, and opportunities for new approaches to interpretation will increase rapidly. New museums should therefore keep in touch with developments in this area, and be aware of the potential that computers have for museum work.

## 4.12 INSURANCE

Insurance is both essential and in some cases compulsory in the museum context. It is also a complicated field and advice from a reputable insurance broker offering independent financial advice on the types of insurance cover needed by the new museum will save time and money in the long term. There are a number of areas of museum work which require or deserve insurance protection:

* personnel - paid and voluntary staff

* visitors

* museum buildings

* collections

* furnishings and fittings

### Staff and visitors

Employers have a duty to provide a safe working environment for their employees under the Health and Safety at Work Act, 1974. There is a compulsory legal requirement on employers to provide Employer's Liability Insurance which protects the employee against injury or illness caused by the employer's negligence. The definition of 'employee' here is a complex one in law, and it is important to define the precise employer/employee relationship when someone is working in or for the museum. Complications can arise where personnel are not full-time employees of the museum, but are temporary or part-time workers.

Volunteers may pose special insurance problems. They would normally be viewed not as employees, but as Third Parties and be covered by Public Liability Insurance. There is however no legal or statutory requirement to provide Public Liability cover. It is

Employers have a duty to provide a safe working environment for their employees.

nonetheless essential to take out insurance cover against injury to volunteers and members of the public as visitors to the museum or in the course of their business.

Where the museum has working machinery or moving vehicles, separate insurance cover will be required. In addition, especially in the case of industrial museums, there may be further statutory liabilities. Third Party insurance is compulsory under the Road Traffic Act where museum vehicles are being driven on the road.

Other areas of insurance which the museum may wish to consider are personal accident and sickness insurance cover for staff and volunteers, health and medical insurance schemes, and pensions and life insurance schemes for staff.

If you are in doubt about any aspect of insurance, seek professional advice. Remember, damage and damages often go together.

### Buildings

Buildings insurance is essential. Where your Governing Body owns museum buildings, it is normally best to take out full rather than limited cover on an indemnity or reinstatement basis. It is also important that the owners of buildings are insured against injury caused by disrepair, such as falling chimneys or slates, under Property Owners' Liability Insurance. Where the buildings are leased or rented, it is usual for the landlord to insure and recharge the tenant accordingly. But, it is imperative to check the landlord's insurance cover carefully, especially where there is a full repairing lease, in case of complications. The landlord may not be insured against damage which you the tenant than have to make good!

Another area of insurance to discuss with your insurance brokers is Business Interruption. Under this category the museum is insured against the loss of revenue income for a defined period of time after a major disaster like flood or fire. It takes time to resume the day-to-day working of a museum after a disaster. Loss of revenue income for the time taken to put the museum to rights can have a serious effect on the museum's operations such as paying staff or bills.

### Collections

The insurance of a museum's collections is made complicated by the difficulties or impossibilities of replacement. However, it is possible and advisable to break down the collections, in store and on display, into different categories. These can then be insured variously on an indemnity basis or at an agreed value. One approach is to have a number of unspecified items and some specified items in the collections covered on an indemnity basis, together with further specified items covered at a value agreed with your insurance company. This provides cover for the whole collection and unique items can be replaced by items of similar quality and interest if disaster should strike. The type and extent of cover will vary depending on the premium paid, and the nature of the risk.

Special care should be taken to ensure that items on loan to other museums/institutions have been separately and comprehensively insured by the borrower. Items on loan to the museum should be insured at a value agreed with the lender. It is also important to ensure that items in transit are fully protected by insurance cover.

Apart from considerable financial embarrassment that any loss or damage can cause, the museum's public image can be badly affected if negligence has taken place through not providing adequate cover for items on loan.

Valuation of collections can be expensive, and the museum should use reputable commercial companies for valuation work. Because prices in the art and antiques market can change quite rapidly, a museum must recognise the need to have regular valuations carried out to ensure that its insurance cover is adequate for the purpose.

### Furnishings and fittings

The value of furnishings, fittings and equipment, together with reference books and shop stock can be considerable. It is advisable to provide insurance cover on an 'all risks' basis to cover any loss or damage. A record or inventory of all equipment and furniture should be kept with a note of the purchase value of all items, which can be updated at regular intervals.

# 5 FURTHER READING

*'Every museum whatever its size should establish a reference library to support its day-to-day work. Keeping up-to-date with museum developments through published material is critically important.'*

## 5.1 MUSEUM REFERENCE LIBRARIES

Every museum whatever its size should establish a reference library to support its day-to-day work. The scale of the library will depend on the size and specialist interests of the museum. A shelf of well-chosen books will be far more useful than an unsystematic collection of out-of-date material. It is essential to identify what priorities should be addressed in terms of acquisitions. A collections management policy for the library is an effective means of ensuring that earmarked resources for library development are targeted at priority areas, and that superseded material is discarded.

In general terms, a reference library will cover all aspects of the museum's operation - museum management, collections management and user services. Material may include textbooks, journals, press-releases and press-cuttings, reports, information sheets, pamphlets, maps, reference books, manufacturers' and suppliers' information, training information and so on. A museum reference library needs to be at least listed and indexed if it is to be used effectively and your investment in it is to be well managed.

In identifying priorities, it is as well to focus on a number of key textbooks and journals about museum work, and a range of standard works concerned with collections and their identification. In addition, a set of standard reference books such as dictionaries, atlases, and publications about the cultural and natural history of the museum's area will be essential. Research and scholarship is an important aspect of the museum's work, and it is essential when providing information to the public to ensure that it is well researched and not derived from out-of-date material.

The checklist below should provide a basic set of publications for a new museum. Developing the reference library should be the responsibility of one individual charged with monitoring new publications and developing the library's holdings in line with the museum's agreed collections management policy. It is often possible to negotiate exchanges of publications if your museum produces its own. It is also worthwhile asking Friends and indeed visitors to help support the library through the donation of publications which may be out of print and difficult to obtain.

Keeping up-to-date with museum developments in museum work is critically important, and regular reading is a powerful method of learning about new developments and approaches relevant to your work. Advice on establishing and developing a museum reference library is available through your Area Museum Council.

Keeping up-to-date with museum developments in museum work is critically important.

## Useful publications

This checklist includes a number of basic textbooks covering a range of different aspects of museum work. Textbooks need to be complemented by journals or periodicals which help to provide information about current developments and reflect current thinking about museum work. A list of key periodicals is provided below.

## Textbooks

Alfrey, J. and Putnam, T. *The Industrial Heritage: Managing Resources and Uses* (London, 1992).

Ambrose, T. *Working with Museums* (Norwich, 1988).

Ambrose, T. and Paine, C. *Museum Basic*s (London, 1993).

Ambrose, T. and Runyard, S. (eds) *Forward Planning: A Handbook of Business, Corporate and Development Planning for Museums and Galleries* (London, 1991).

Belcher, M. *Exhibitions in Museums* (Leicester, 1991).

Durbin, G., Morris, S., and Wilkinson, S. *A Teacher's Guide to Learning from Objects* (London, 1985).

Fleming, D., Paine, C., and Rhodes, J. (eds) *Social History in Museums* (London, 1993).

Guldbeck, P.E. and MacLeish, A.B. (eds) *The Care of Antiques and Historical Collections* (Nashville, 1985).

Hoare, N. *Security for Museums* (Committee of Area Museum Councils, 1990).

Hooper-Greenhill, E. *Initiatives in Museum Education* (Leicester, 1989).

Hooper-Greenhill, E. *Museum and Gallery Education* (Leicester, 1991).

Hooper-Greenhill, E. *Writing a Museum Education policy* (Leicester, 1991).

International Council of Museums (ICOM) *ICOM Statutes and Code of Professional Ethics* (Paris, 1990).

International Council of Museums (ICOM) *Museum Security* (London, 1992).

Kavanagh, G. (ed) *Museum Languages - Objects and Texts* (Leicester, 1991).

Kavanagh, G. (ed) *The Museums Profession: Internal and External Relations* (Leicester, 1991).

Kavanagh, G. *History Curatorship* (Leicester, 1990).

Lord, B., Lord, G., and Hicks, J. *The Cost of Collecting - Collection Management in UK Museums* (London, 1989).

Lord, B., and Lord, G. *The Manual of Museum Planning* (Norwich, 1991).

Merriman, N. *Beyond the Glass Case: the Past, the Heritage and the Public in Britain* (Leicester, 1991).

Middleton, V. *New Visions for Independent Museums* (Association of Independent Museums, 1990).

Millar, S. *Volunteers in Museums and Heritage Organisations* (Norwich, 1991).

Museums and Galleries Commission *Guidelines for a Registration Scheme for Museums in the UK* (London, 1987).

Museums and Galleries Commission *Standards in the Museum Care of Collections - 1. Archaeological Collections (1992). 2. Biological Collections (1993). 3. Geological Collections (1993).*

Museums and Galleries Commission *Environmental Management Guidelines* (London, 1993).

Museums and Galleries Commission *Guidelines on Disability for Museums and Galleries* (London, 1992).

Museums and Galleries Commission *Quality of Service in Museums and Galleries: Customer Care in Museums, Guidelines on Implementation* (London, 1992).

Pearce, S. (ed) *Museum Studies in Material Culture* (Leicester, 1989).

Pearce, S. *Archaeological Curatorship* (Leicester, 1990).

Roberts, A.D. *Collections Management for Museums* (Cambridge, 1988).

Sandwith, H., and Stainton, S. *The National Trust Manual of Housekeeping* (Harmondsworth, 1984).

Thomson, G. *The Museum Environment* (London, 1986).

Thompson, J.M.A. (ed) *Manual of Curatorship* (London, 1992).

Thompson, P. *The Voice of the Past: Oral History* (Oxford, 1988).

Velarde, G. *Designing Exhibitions* (London, 1988).

## Journals and Periodicals

There is a very wide range of journals and periodicals available for those working in museums and allied areas, such as tourism and leisure. All Area Museum Councils will provide regular bulletins for their members, and specialist groups within the museums profession such as the Group for Education in Museums or the Museum Professionals Group produce their own journals. Guidance on titles can be obtained through your Area Museum Council and through the Museums Yearbook (see below).

*Museums Journal* is published monthly by the Museums Association (see section 6.0) and is the main UK professional journal for all those working in museums.

*Museum Abstracts* is published monthly by the Scottish Museums Council (see section 6.0) and serves as a primary source of information on published material in the fields of administration and finance, collecting and collections management, conservation and restoration, educational activities, exhibition design and display, legislation policy, marketing and visitor services, planning and development, theory and methodology, and training and professional development.

*AIM Bulletin* is published bi-monthly by the Association of Independent Museums (see section 6.0) and is an important source of information for all those working in independent museums.

*Museums Yearbook* is published by the Museums Association (see section 6.0), annually. It contains a complete listing of all the museums in the UK with their staff, information on Area Museum Councils, specialist groups, Regional Museum Federations, related organisations, and training courses together with an extensive listing of products and services for museums from manufacturers, suppliers and consultants. It also includes the Code of Conduct for Museum Professionals, the Code of Practice for Museum Authorities, Guidelines for Committee Members, Guidelines on Performance Measurement in museums, and the Museums and Galleries Commission/Museums Association Guidelines on Disability for Museums and Galleries. Further information includes international museums associations and contacts, and a list of personal members of the Museums Association. It is essential reading for all those involved in museums in whatever capacity.

*ICOM News* is published quarterly by the International Council of Museums (see section 6.0) and is a useful source of information providing an international perspective on museum activities.

# 6 OTHER SOURCES OF INFORMATION

*'No museum is an island, and every museum can benefit from advice and information from other museums and allied organisations.'*

The main sources of information for those managing new museums are given below. However, for further information on organisations available to support your work and details of names and addresses etc., you should refer to the Museums Association's *Museums Yearbook* and your Area Museum Council.

### Area Museum Councils

**Yorkshire and Humberside Museums Council**, Farnley Hall, Hall Lane, Leeds LS12 5HA. Tel. 0532 638909/633092; fax 791479.

**Area Museum Council for the South West**, Hestercombe House, Cheddon Fitzpaine, Taunton TA2 8LQ. Tel. 0823 259696; fax 413114.

**Area Museums Service for South Eastern England**, Ferroners House, Barbican, London EC2Y 8AA. Tel. 071 600 0219; fax 600 2581.

**The Council of Museums in Wales**, 32 Park Place, Cardiff CF1 3BA. Tel. 0222 225432/228238; fax 668516.

**East Midlands Museums Service**, Courtyard Buildings, Wollaton Park, Nottingham, NG8 2AE. Tel. 0602 854534; fax 280038.

**North of England Museums Service**, House of Recovery, Bath Lane, Newcastle-upon-Tyne NE4 5SQ. Tel. 091 222 1661; fax 261 4725.

**North West Museum Service**, Griffin Lodge, Cavendish Place, Blackburn BB2 2PN. Tel. 0254 670211; fax 681995.

**Scottish Museums Council**, County House, 20-22 Torphichen Street, Edinburgh EH3 8JB. Tel. 031 229 7465; fax 229 2728.

**West Midlands Area Museum Service**, Hanbury Road, Stoke Prior, Bromsgrove, Worcestershire. Tel. 0527 72258; fax 576960.

**Northern Ireland Museums Council**, 185 Stranmillis Road, Belfast BT9 5DU. Tel. 0232 661023; fax 661715.

### Other organisations

**Association of Independent Museums (AIM)**, Weald and Downland Museum, Singleton, West Sussex. Tel. 0744 21515; fax 0704 22599.

**British Association of Friends of Museums (BAFM)**, 548 Wilbraham Road, Manchester M21 1LB.

**International Council of Museums (ICOM)**, Maison de l'Unesco, 1 rue Miollis, 75732 Paris Cedex 15, France. Tel. 47 34 05 00.

**Museums Association (MA)**, 42 Clerkenwell Close, London EC1R 0PA. Tel. 071 608 2933.

**Museums and Galleries Commission (MGC)**, 16 Queen Anne's Gate, London SW1H 9AA. Tel. 071 233 4200; fax 233 3686.

**Museum Training Institute (MTI)**, Kershaw House, 55 Well Street, Bradford, West Yorkshire BD1 5PS. Tel. 0274 391056/087/092; fax 394890.

**Museum Documentation Association (MDA)**, Lincoln House, 347 Cherry Hinton Road, Cambridge CB1 4DH. Tel. 0223 242848; fax 213575.

# INDEX

Printed by HMSO, Edinburgh Press
Dd 0287943 C30 10/93 (215376)

 **HMSO**

HMSO publications are available from:

**HMSO Publications Centre**
(Mail, fax and telephone orders only)
PO Box 276, London, SW8 5DT
Telephone orders 071-873 9090
General enquiries 071-873 0011
(queuing system in operation for both numbers)
Fax orders 071-873 8200

**HMSO Bookshops**
71 Lothian Road, Edinburgh, EH3 9AZ
031-228 4181 Fax 031-229 2734
49 High Holborn, London, WC1V 6HB
071-873 0011 Fax 071-873 8200 (counter service only)
258 Broad Street, Birmingham, B1 2HE
021-643 3740 Fax 021-643 6510
33 Wine Street, Bristol, BS1 2BQ
0272 264306 Fax 0272 294515
9-21 Princess Street, Manchester, M60 8AS
061-834 7201 Fax 061-833 0634
16 Arthur Street, Belfast, BT1 4GD
0232 238451 Fax 0232 235401

**HMSO's Accredited Agents**
(see Yellow Pages)

*and through good booksellers*